and learn from. This is a story of triumph and family; laughter and healing; and courage and perseverance."

—GAIL R.

"This book is simply wonderful. It was touching and humorous in all the right ways. As a person in the healthcare profession and a woman, this book was a must read for me."

—TIMILY H.

"Both witty and moving at the same time, Maryellen shares her personal feelings in regards to her diagnosis as well as the intimate details of her doctors appointments and everything in between. Her refreshing and entertaining outlook on her diagnosis makes the book easy to read and hard to put down."

—AMY M.

"I cannot pinpoint the precise alchemy that went into making Maryellen's book so pitch perfect. I sat down one busy afternoon to simply look over Maryellen's book to see what it was like. I read the first paragraph of the first page and never stopped until I was finished. How does someone so young, in the prime of their life, with three children and a husband counting on them to live find themselves facing a mortal danger?

If you are Maryellen, you do it with grace and humor and strength of character."
—EILEEN B.

"This is a refreshing and honest account of real life with breast cancer. The ups and downs of how life and relationships endure the 'Breast cancer challenge.' Maryellen's 'snip-its' of so many aspects of her journey are fun and easy to read. I couldn't put it down, and can't help but to share it! Even my husband loved it! A great gift for anyone touched by Breast Cancer... it's the 'real deal!'"
—CATHY R.

"This book simply chronicles a woman's life from diagnosis of breast cancer through completion of treatment and beyond. It is a heartfelt journey with sensitivity as well as humor. The author puts procedures into layman's terms and challenges the medical profession to remember the need to be patient focused. It praises where praise is due, it critiques when criticism may lead to growth. Humor and a positive outlook are the common thread weaving the story together to its hopeful completion. I highly recommend this book to all patients, families, caregivers, and loved ones of cancer patients. I guess that's EVERYONE...until we find a cure."
—FRANCES L.

Why I Hated Pink

Confessions of a Breast Cancer Survivor

• MARYELLEN D. BRISBOIS •

vantage
POINT

Published by Vantage Point Books

Vantage Press, Inc.

419 Park Avenue South

New York, NY 10016

www.vantagepointbooks.com

Manufactured in the United States of America

ISBN: 978-1-936467-01-3

Library of Congress Cataloging-in-Publication data is on file.

0   9   8   7   6   5   4   3   2   1

Cover and Interior design by Pauline Neuwirth.

"Courage is being scared to death and saddling up anyway."

—JOHN WAYNE 1907–1979

author's note

The names and other identifying characteristics of some persons included in this memoir have been changed.

kudos

*T*he writing of this memoir would not have been possible without the support and encouragement of many inspiring people in my life who thought my story was worth telling.

I extend my love to my husband Brian and gratitude to my children Travis, Tyler, and Mackenzie for making my life complete.

I cannot put into words my appreciation of my amazing family and friends who knew me well enough to keep my life "business as usual" and for always knowing what I needed before I did.

Special thanks to the doctors, nurses, and staff who carried me through some pretty trying days; and for those breast cancer patients who came before me to light the way with their courage and determination.

My story would not have been told with any humor had it not been for my father, who showed me by example how to face a challenge with extraordinary grace and dignity.

To my sister Erin, who is a tireless source of quiet support in all of my endeavors.

—Maryellen D. Brisbois

"*A*re you sitting down?"

That's what the nurse practitioner said as I picked up the phone early one December morning in 2006. They really say that to people. It's not just in the movies! I had a biopsy a few days earlier to determine if the "cyst" in my breast was the real thing. The cyst that had apparently been benign for the last three years, the cyst that didn't reveal anything ominous on the previous three million mammograms I'd had. That "cyst."

"No, I'm not sitting down," I said, "but I know what you're going to tell me."

"I really think you should sit down."

"I can't," I said. "I'm looking for a stinking pen to write down what you're about to tell me."

This phone call was going to change my life. I knew it before I picked up the phone. The nurse told me that they had found atypical cells in the breast biopsy pathology results and that I needed an MRI and core biopsy as soon as possible.

"Thanks," I said.

"Are you ok?"

"I'm fine, just fine."

I hung up the phone and envisioned a million things. As a nurse for over twenty years, most of what I envisioned was not good. I had just turned forty-one.

· mri ·

 $\mathcal{S}$ ometimes no information is a good thing. Sometimes, though, we deserve a good heads up so we know what the hell to expect. I never thought I'd find myself in an MRI machine lying on my stomach with breasts hanging toward the floor in cone-like compartments. A man must have invented such a thing. A woman would have to be a gymnast to get on the contraption in the first place.

After I took a deep breath, the MRI itself was easy. Once the intravenous (IV) was in I just had to lie still. *No sweat, I thought. I'm too scared to move anyway.* When I drove myself to the MRI that morning, I knew the results were not going to be good. Now, you may think I'm crazy, but as I drove to the hospital, I saw a sign for the hospital on the right-hand side of the highway. To my left, a car drove by with a breast cancer ribbon magnet on it. Bad karma, whether you believe in that stuff or not.

· surgeon ·

I first saw a breast surgeon three years ago because of "dense breast tissue." I was told it was nothing. I became vigilant, keeping all of my appointments for mammograms and ultrasounds. Vigilant. October is breast cancer awareness month. I began to wonder, *is this all in my head?*

I called my sister-in-law for advice. She's an OR nurse. She put me in contact with a different surgeon to see the next day. But I had to get my MRI films first. No sweat.

I was teaching nursing students that semester at a local college. I gave the evaluations to the students without breaking *down*, ran to get the MRI films, and buzzed back to see the surgeon in what seemed like an hour.

· cyst ·

The surgeon examined me and said not to worry. The cyst, which later was named "The Fucker" by my younger sister Linda, was nothing, he said. He proceeded to put my MRI disc into the computer. Suddenly, colors bloomed on the computer screen. He told me that the cyst was breast cancer and discussed some treatment/surgery options. I was alone when I went to the visit because the appointment had been scheduled so quickly. I never thought to bring reinforcements. Bad idea.

On my way out of the office, I paused at the desk to schedule my next appointment. The waiting room walls were filled with large photographs of breast cancer survivors. The surgeon remarked, "Lots of people are diagnosed near the holidays. When the people in these pictures die, we just put up new ones."

I felt better already! Why don't people just stop talking sometimes?

As I was on my way home, my husband called my cell phone.

"It's cancer," I said.

"Oh no."

He told me weeks later that he felt awful that he hadn't been with me to hear the news. Little did we know the fun was about to begin.

· scans ·

I was paired with an oncologist. I loved her instantly. We chatted, and she gave me the rundown on how the next several months would play out. Yes, I did say months. Four months of chemotherapy, then surgery, then seven weeks of radiation. Followed by five years of the medication Tamoxifen in oral form. Great!

Before anything could progress, I had to have further tests. Many tests. I hate tests. As a nurse, I was now on the other side of this story. I had been foolish to think I knew anything about what cancer patients were going through. The words *oncology unit* now took my breath away, before, they were just letters on a sign.

I had a CT scan of my chest and abdomen to be sure The Fucker had not spread. I also had a bone scan for the same reason.

A MUGA scan also had to be performed to check the condition of my heart, because the chemotherapy would wreak havoc on every bit of me. Hopefully, The Fucker would get the brunt of it. Hopefully.

I sat waiting for my CT scan, sipping the contrast drink. It was gross. I pictured myself in the Caribbean sipping a fruity drink. It helped a little.

· biopsies ·

I had to have a core biopsy done. The results of this biopsy would tell us more about the tumor and what treatment was appropriate. My husband accompanied me and stayed with me throughout the procedure. The nurse who stayed with me was magnificent.

The doctor talked a blue streak about how the MRI was wrong and that what he could palpate was clearly *not* cancer. He was so sure he was right, he forgot to put a marker in while doing the biopsy. As a result, I was confused and doubtful. I had to have the marker inserted at a later time because of his prior omission. The biopsy showed cancer: Stage II invasive ductal carcinoma. Shit.

· me ·

I was blindsided. I had no risk factors for breast cancer. I was an avid runner and had been for the last twenty-seven years. I had completed a triathlon, in addition to many, many road races and a couple of half marathons under my belt. I ate right, rarely drank (except for my annual Christmas party and girls' weekend), and had only gained a few pounds since high school. My dad's sister had a lump removed several years ago and my maternal great aunt had a mastectomy many years before she died but the details were quite sketchy. Why me?

"Bad luck," my beloved oncologist said. No kidding. I never thought of myself as having bad luck, more like dumb luck. I had a great husband, kids, and family. I had the best, best friends a woman could ask for. And I loved being a nurse. I'd been a nurse for twenty-one years. I was even going for my master's degree and would finish in a few months.

Bad luck? I guess you could say that. I have never won the lottery. The last time I *won* something was in second grade. But even on my worst day, I never thought of myself as having bad luck. Where do I go from here? I'm a doer and needed answers and a plan.

· team meeting ·

I had a scheduled team meeting with the medical oncologist, nurse, NP, radiation oncologist, and surgeon. It was on December 22nd. Merry Christmas. My husband and I left the house early for the meeting.

On the way to the hospital, we stopped at K-Mart for a tape recorder. It was a last minute decision to stop. We thought a tape recorder would be a great thing to bring along to be sure we didn't miss any pertinent information. A kid in K-Mart helped us find a tape recorder, but gave us the wrong tapes to play in it. We were so nervous, that we didn't realize the mistake until we tore the recorder out of the package while racing to the meeting. When we threw the batteries in it, we realized that the tape didn't fit. Thankfully, I had a pen and a lot of paper!

I envisioned the meeting taking place in a beautiful board room with a mahogany table and silk drapes, all eyes on me as specialists hung on my every word. I ended up being in an exam room wearing a hospital gown with my breasts exposed most of the time while being hammered with so much information that I couldn't absorb another word. It was surreal.

· shrinkage ·

We discussed the potential benefits of having chemotherapy first, hoping to avoid a mastectomy. I agreed. I had always thought that I wouldn't care if my breasts were lopped off; I figured it would be okay, but I was wrong. It was a big deal, and it was worth trying the chemo first. The oncologist said that in rare cases, the chemotherapy would destroy the whole tumor. I knew better. Remember, I'm the girl with the bad luck!

Each doctor had his or her own spiel that day and told me their piece of the treatment puzzle. I was overwhelmed and exhausted. I had many questions. The most important one was: "Can I please have chemo on Thursdays so I feel well enough to finish my master's degree classes on Mondays and Wednesdays?"

"Of course," my medical oncologist said with a smile.

I was smitten. When I reached the car, I cried and apologized to my husband for dragging him through all of this. The tears surprised me.

· slip sliding away ·

*I*t is amazing how you feel fear. I can only liken the fear that I endured to driving in a snowstorm and the feeling in your chest when you realize that you have lost control of the car. The difference was that the feeling in my chest didn't go away. As treatment ended and I resumed a somewhat normal routine, it left as quickly as it had come.

· couch ·

I'd be lying if I said I wasn't scared shitless, although I *am* known for being strong, almost to a fault. I face everything head-on. I wasn't so sure about this, though. This might be even too big for me.

I'm also a lousy sleeper. I can be awake for hours at a time, thinking of silly things that seem insurmountable at night, but are nothing when the sun comes up. But cancer was big!

My husband, Brian, on the other hand, can always sleep. I often sneak out of bed in the middle of the night to watch T.V. or read and try not to wake him. After the diagnosis, we'd race each other to get to the couch at bedtime. Sleep eluded us. We held hands and pretended that our lives were normal and that the sudden need to watch the news every morning at 4 a.m. was not unusual.

The hardest times were waiting for results. It seemed like every long weekend meant I was waiting for test results. It was awful.

Our couch party lasted for a couple of weeks. We would pick up our pillows and blankets from the couch before the kids woke up for school. That craziness ended when I found the courage to ask my primary doctor for something to help me sleep. I counted on him many more times in the days to come. He never let me down.

· bomb ·

*O*ne of the worst things I had to face with a cancer diagnosis was telling my friends and family. I felt so badly that I had to tell them, and then they had to live with the news as well as with me. Spreading the news exhausted me.

We have three children. At that time, Travis was a junior in high school, Tyler was a freshman, and Mackenzie (Kenzie) was a sixth grader. Brian and I waited a few days before telling the kids. We decided that after Christmas would be best. Why ruin their holiday, too? We did, however, tell our siblings, my mother, and his parents. My three nursing school buddies also got the news pre-holiday. They took the news harder than I did. Much harder. I always believed that I was going to be okay and I had started to feel fearless. Totally fearless. I was going to ride this wave of fearlessness until it ran out!

I spread the news as well as I could, staying positive and upbeat. I told people based on whether I would want to know firsthand if something happened to them. For those people, I called with the news so they wouldn't hear it through the grapevine. Everyone knew that the kids would not be told until after Christmas but sometimes even the best-laid plans have holes in them.

I was dropping off something at my in-laws a couple of days after my husband had told his parents about my diagnosis. When they saw me, my mother-in-law yelled, "I love you like my own!" She was crying. Tyler was right behind me. I had no choice but to tell the boys. The revised plan was not to tell Kenzie until after the holidays. I figured that if I could pull it off, everyone else should be able to.

· boys ·

$\mathcal{T}$yler is my sensitive son. Even as a teenager, he asked me a million times a day if he could do anything for me. After the outburst at my in-laws, Tyler asked me if someone had died. I said no, and that I would tell him what was going on after school. Everything was fine, I assured him.

That afternoon, the boys got off the bus together. I waited for them as they came up the driveway. I honestly prayed that I would die of a heart attack before they got to the door. I didn't die. All those years of running had made my heart too strong. Telling the boys was one of the hardest things I would ever have to do in my life. Ever.

About three weeks before my diagnosis, my neighbor died of breast cancer. She had battled the disease for many years. She left a husband and three sons who were in the same grades as my boys. Her death was a huge loss to our community. My news had to be told on the heels of her passing. Not well known for my tact I was going to give it my best shot.

· proud ·

On one of the worst days of my life, I couldn't have been more proud. I explained the diagnosis and treatment to my sons. I told them that I had a great prognosis and that the surgeon had told me that I would live a long life. In my best and strongest voice, I said it would be "business as usual" around the house and that this was no excuse for slipping grades in school. I said we may need some help from time to time, but that in a few months, I'd be back at the top of my game.

The boys never took their eyes off of me. They never sat. Both Travis and Tyler looked as if the gears were spinning in their heads. They asked about the risks to their little sister, while assuring each other that by the time Kenzie grew up, medicine would be so advanced that nothing would be the same. They stated that we didn't need outside help and promised to cook and clean. They made *me* promise that I would always tell them the truth about what was going on, even if the news was bad. I was dumbfounded and proud. I agreed to always tell the truth and told them they could ask me whatever questions they had. They promised to keep the news from Kenzie until the holidays were over.

· holidays ·

I suppose the holidays went off without a hitch. I felt like an actress in a horror film. Brian was best supporting actor. Only there was no red carpet, no Vera Wang gown, no up-dos, and no trophies.

We went to my sister and her husband's house on Christmas Eve and had a great evening. My nephew Michael told me that cancer had met its match.

Everyone had a good time, and I slowly let myself enjoy the holidays a bit. The big event of the night was when a bat flew into the living room of Karen and Bob's beautiful Victorian home. Everyone screamed and laughed.

Christmas Day at my in-laws was busy and went by quickly. We made it through.

· kenzie ·

The kids were on holiday vacation. Kenzie slept in the day after Christmas. The boys whispered and wondered when I was going to tell her. They looked as nervous as I felt. I hoped for a fatal heart attack, but nothing happened. I climbed the stairs to her room as slowly as I could. I climbed into her bed and told her the news. I got mad at myself for crying. I asked her if she had questions. She asked if I'd lose my hair, and I said that I would. I repeated what I had said to her brothers. We headed downstairs and I gave the boys a "thumbs up" as we passed them.

An hour later, Kenzie came into the kitchen where I was doing dishes. She had a question for me. She wanted to know if I would get a wig. Apparently, she envisioned me being so defiant about losing my hair that I'd walk around bald. I promised that I would get a wig. She was satisfied and left to play with her gifts.

· obits ·

I drove Kenzie to the bus each morning and took the newspaper along. One morning, Kenzie asked who was the oldest person on the obituary page. Every morning after that, we looked for the oldest person. There was comfort in this game, reading that many people do live long lives.

· father ·

My father was one of those men to whom people flocked. He had a great sense of humor. He had presence. I adored him.

My Dad loved to work and yard work was no exception. He mowed the grass in perfect patterns. We often joked that his yard looked better than Fenway Park.

My father died the year that Kenzie was born. Before he died, we had a pretty frank talk about life and death. I asked him to look out for the kids if he was able to after he died. He promised that he would. We laughed about him knocking cigarettes out of their hands if they started smoking when they were teenagers. He laughed at what was funny, even when he knew how sick he was.

After he died, I used to tell the kids that Grandpa was mowing the grass in heaven. They were little and they thought that mowing grass in heaven was a perfect job for their grandfather.

I was surprised when I found myself a little miffed at my father after being diagnosed with breast cancer. I laughed that he must be off with a couple of leggy blondes and forgot to watch out for us. I had been so grateful to have had such a headstrong and influential guardian angel.

· media ·

If you want to buy a new car, you see the car you want all over the road and on television ads. With a fresh breast cancer diagnosis, every other commercial seemed to be about breast cancer walks, shampoos, or cancer centers. We couldn't even sit down as a family to watch T.V. without the constant reminder.

Pink apparel was everywhere! Pink had been my favorite color since I was very little. The hotter the shade, the more I liked it. But I began hating pink, hating pink ribbons, and feeling the need for a new favorite color.

There were also continued reports of breast cancer research. One day eating red meat might be the cause, while the next day eating red meat was the prevention. I was confused about what guidelines to follow so I decided to do as I had always done: Keep everything in moderation.

My treatment moved along smoothly, and the cancer advertisements slowed down. Crazy how that works.

· brian ·

I have *never* met anyone who didn't speak highly of my husband. Ever! He is mellow and kind. He works hard for his family everyday without complaint. He loves his children. He is honest and fair.

He and I met in 1983, when we enrolled in a diploma nursing school program in the heart of Worcester. We were friends and drinking buddies before we started dating a couple of years later. We married in 1988. We dreamed of little "Brisbois" and knew, as nurses, that we'd probably work opposite shifts for years so one of us would almost always be home with the kids.

On our first anniversary, I was five months pregnant and in my early twenties. We worked hard and were happy. Brian's Mom told us that we couldn't live on love, but we proved her wrong. Travis was born and we were wildly crazy about him. We spent tons of time with him. We hoped, as every parent does, that he'd be a great man. We wanted great things for our little guy.

Twenty-two months later, Tyler arrived on a cold winter morning. A brother for Travis! Tyler was dark haired in contrast to his brother's fairness. He looked like Ernie from *Sesame Street*. He was a blessing, and we adored our boys. We were so pleased to have another son.

Kenzie arrived three years later. To have a little girl after having two boys was a blessing. She was a wonderful, easy baby. She had to be.

· meeting ·

When Kenzie was seven days old, my father called to say that he and my mother were coming over.

"Please call your sisters and brother and have them meet us at your house," he said.

He had been battling leukemia for five years and he hadn't been doing very well in recent weeks.

That day, he told us he was stopping all treatment and was expected to live about three months. Devastated does not begin to describe how I felt, and how we all felt. He was fifty-five years old.

· turning point ·

*M*y life changed after my father was diagnosed with cancer. I was a new mother to Travis when Brian came home with the news that my father had leukemia. Brian had unexpectedly run into my parents as they left the hospital following their appointment.

The effect of the news was devastating, and my life was never the same. I felt safe when my dad was around. I never thought he wouldn't be there. I hoped that my children would not be affected by the news of my diagnosis as I was when I heard about my father. They seemed to withstand the news differently than I did, and it didn't seem like they were, but I am not sure if my father knew how his news on that October day in 1990 changed so many things about me.

· eleven ·

*W*hen I was eleven years old, we packed up the Ford station wagon and drove an hour heading westward down the Mass Pike to exit three to my grandmother's house for Thanksgiving. My parents, three sisters, brother, and I crammed together in the car. Seven passengers .

We kids fought and Dad would swing his arm around to the back seat to swat at us and yell, "Don't make me stop this car!"

I also had severe motion sickness. Even a short ride made me sick. My father kept bags under the seat of the car just in case. He hated to stop for anything, never mind a vomiting kid. My mother would mutter, "Oh, Maryellen." I hated to ride in the car. My siblings didn't want to ride with me after I was sick either, so I got elbowed and shoved until we arrived at our destination.

This particular Thanksgiving stands out. I had a shag haircut that I regretted the minute I left the barber chair. I wore a green turtleneck and floral overalls. Ugly brown shoes rounded out my Thanksgiving outfit.

I lay on the floor watching television with my cousins. We had tons of wonderful cousins, aunts, and uncles. I felt lumps in my flat chest because I was entering puberty. I thought I had breast cancer. I was terrified. I calmed down a few days later when I talked myself out of breast cancer and figured that my body was just changing. That same terror spread through me thirty years later like a freight train.

· plastic surgeon ·

One of my appointments was with a plastic surgeon. Brian was with me, and the surgeon was kind. I recall little of the appointment, except that he had me stand on the step of the exam table topless. He explained what might happen if I needed a mastectomy. Insurance would cover any cosmetic surgery. He spoke about nipple reconstruction, tram flaps, and the like. He said that he could make a 'new nipple' out of tissue from my labia. *My labia!*

A woman who accompanied him was very nice as well. She was a cancer survivor. She had had many positive lymph nodes and had survived for more than fifteen years. Stories about survival made me breathe easier. I began to love a good survival story.

We left the office, still unsure about how invasive my surgery would be. The surgeon said to call anytime with any questions.

Brain and I laughed all the way home about the labia transplant.

· topless ·

I had many appointments in those first weeks after the diagnosis. My breasts were examined by oncologists, surgeons, medical residents, nurse practitioners, and janitors. Just kidding! I told the doctors that one day I was going to walk into the hospital topless. They thought I was crazy. I thought I was funny.

I heard the story of another patient who walked in with a sign stating her name and date of birth, because every time she came into the clinic, staff asked her for her name and date of birth. She was a woman after my own heart.

One of the medical residents was very sweet, and was doing a rotation at the cancer center and I told her that she was brave to go through that particular rotation with breast cancer patients.

"No," she said. "You're the brave one."

· opinion ·

I am a firm believer in a second opinion, so we decided to take a ride into Boston. The ride into the city went well and I hadn't spent this much time with my husband in years.

We stopped on the way for a quick bite to eat at one of those food court–gas station combos. My husband knows how to treat a girl! I grabbed a couple of slices of pizza and found a seat at the last table. An elderly couple approached and asked if they could share the table with me. "Sure," I said.

As Brian approached with his food, he looked at me, disapproving. He sat down without a word.

The couple was on their way to a local clinic. They looked tired and worried. We made small talk while we ate our lunch. For days later, this scenario struck both Brian and me as funny. While I love talking to people, Brian is much quieter. I often think about that couple and hope they are well. I imagine our paths crossed for a reason.

My appointment was uneventful. The doctor agreed with every treatment that was proposed and said it would be easier to receive treatment closer to home.

We couldn't get out of there fast enough. We had waited two hours to see the oncologist there and were anxious to escape. All of the patients had matching wigs, identification bracelets, and sallow faces. I felt so healthy and never imagined that I could look like that.

· time ·

I realized pretty quickly that cancer is time consuming. With appointments and traveling, much of my time was swallowed up by a disease that I never thought I'd have. Waiting rooms were full of people, just waiting. I hated my time being wasted. I hated being rushed if I had questions.

I asked several of the doctors how long they thought I'd had the cancer. One said several years; another said that I may have had it for up to ten years. Ten years. I thought, *If I could accomplish all that I did in my life with cancer, just imagine what I could do without it.*

· shopping ·

On our way home from the second opinion, we stopped at the wig store. I was advised to shop for a wig before chemo, so the wig would match my hairstyle and color. I was nauseated at the idea of needing a wig.

We decided on a wig with help from the owners. They put a skin-colored skullcap over my hair and I tried different wigs. I couldn't get out of the salon fast enough. After it arrived, I went back for a wig cut. Will this craziness ever end?

As I put the wig over my soon-to-be-gone hair, the shop owner gasped and asked if I had worked as a nurse in the ICU in 1987.

"Yes," I responded.

He remembered my face because I spoke to him in the ICU when his dad was really ill. He said he would never forget what I said to him.

Shit, I thought, *what did I say to him?*

He said that his father was recovering from open-heart surgery, and his condition had worsened. I told him that sometimes no matter what we do to save people, it was out of our control and in the hands of a higher power. My words brought his family comfort that day. I worked in the ICU for one year. I'm glad what I said helped him.

On my way out of the shop with my brand-new wig on its Styrofoam head in a plastic bag, I said to the shop owner over my shoulder, "I was much cuter back then."

I planned on stopping for an oil change on my way home, but laughed because I had the wig on the Styrofoam head on the front seat and didn't have the breath to tell my story should the mechanic ask.

· francie ·

*M*y friend Francie is one of my NSBs or nursing school buddies. We've been friends since the early 80s. I can't think of a better friend in the world. Francie is the sensitive type; she is empathetic and sweet. She's also one of the first friends I told about my diagnosis.

One day, while the gates of hell were flooding me with information and my head was spinning, Francie called to check in and say hello. She had no idea how the conversation would turn out. When I told her my diagnosis, she pulled her car off the highway and cried. Her words were positive, but tears were in her voice.

Francie promised to call our other NSBs, Cathy and Monique (Moke). I appreciated her generosity because it was so difficult to tell people over and over again about my pending four months of chemotherapy, followed possibly by surgery, and seven weeks of radiation.

Francie and I decided to meet the next day at TJ Maxx to browse and gab. I told her that she had to suck it up if she wanted to meet me, because I couldn't stand anyone being "down" around me. Being sensitive, I didn't know if she had it in her to not cry. But she surprised me and kept tabs on my every appointment. She listened to me complain and cry, and she always called back to check on me.

Throughout the whole ordeal, I learned how important friends are and how lucky I am to have the friends that I do.

· results ·

*T*he results of my scans and biopsies came in and the news was all good. The scans were done primarily for diagnosis, staging, and to see if anything had metastasized or spread to other parts of my body. It was nerve-wracking and the tests began on December 26th. I went by myself because I never waited long, and it was useless to have someone meet me. I preferred to save the company for my chemotherapy treatments.

My sister Erin came with me for the bone scan, because there was a two-hour lapse between the dye injection and the actual procedure. We spent the time at the mall. I appreciated everyone's offer of company, but it didn't make sense to waste everyone's time.

· grown men telling me they love me ·

The news hit the men in my life pretty hard. Out of nowhere, these men told me they loved me. I wasn't sure I liked it. Maybe they put themselves in my husband's place and felt sympathetic. Maybe they really love me!

My brother-in-law, Don, was one of the first. He e-mailed me a note saying that I had to beat the cancer and that he loved me. Next was my father-in-law, possibly the quietest man I have ever met. I adore him. My brother followed suit, and I do not ever recall him telling me that he loved me. Hell, I knew he did, we just never said it to each other.

· words of wisdom and a flu shot ·

I saw my primary doctor for a flu shot and pneumonia shot before starting chemo. He may be the sweetest doctor I have known. He is thoughtful, and listens to what I tell him.

He told me, on that cold December day, that I was his favorite patient and that he loved me. He told me to try not to listen to statistics about survival and to live my life one day at a time. His words helped me get through some long and tedious appointments. He said if I ever needed to cry, he would be there for me because he knew I'd want to be strong for everyone else. He is a great man.

· tracks of my tears ·

I would drive along the road or take a walk or do dishes and my eyes would just tear up. Tears would run down my cheeks. I wasn't particularly sad, but I couldn't stop the tears. My eyes just ran. The tears lasted for many months and as I ended my treatment, they stopped. I was back to my usual, non-crying self.

· nighttime phone calls ·

I read a magazine article about cancer while in a waiting room at the hospital. The only magazines available were about cancer. Trust me when I tell you that *any* other magazine would be a welcome distraction when waiting for a test, diagnosis, or prognosis.

One article in the cancer magazine, however, made me smile. It was a story about how once people are diagnosed with cancer, they should be given a list of people from another country on the other side of the world that they could call in the middle of the night and just complain and rattle on about how life sucked. Because I still wasn't sleeping, I spent so much time awake with my mind reeling. The beauty of the article was that the person called didn't even have to speak the same language. It would be cathartic in the middle of the night to speak to another human that didn't have to be woken up.

· cathy and moke ·

*C*athy and Moke, my other two NSBs, have been my friends since 1983. We endured nursing school, our dating years, marriage, pregnancy, childbirth, childrearing, career issues, family obligations, and everything in between.

Cathy was my roommate in nursing school. Moke lived a couple of doors down the hall in our very strict Catholic nursing school dorm. We have millions of stories and memories and when we get together, we talk and laugh for hours.

· dinner and a photo shoot ·

My NSBs and I met for dinner at a halfway point between our homes at least every couple of months. This one time, I was the elephant in the room. But in spite of my new diagnosis, we ended up having a good evening.

We stopped into a store and shopped for hats for my impending baldness.

I had my camera in the car and we decided to get a picture of the four of us. We walked into a store and asked a young worker in the store if he would take our picture.

"Sure," he said, "Sit down on the display couch and I'll get a few shots."

We laughed at how he didn't even flinch when we asked him. I look awful in the picture because I had a stress rash on my neck and looked like hell. I loved that we were together doing something simple.

· housekeepers ·

*B*rian and the kids started cleaning the house on Saturday mornings without being asked. Without being asked!

There was a flurry of activity: bed linens changed, floors vacuumed and mopped, and furniture dusted. They drew the line at cleaning bathrooms. The bathroom cleaning was still my job. This cleaning extravaganza lasted throughout my entire chemo treatment. I fall apart if my house is a mess! They knew I had bigger things to worry about.

· kelley tuthill ·

*a*round this time, I learned that a newscaster from our local T.V. station had been diagnosed with breast cancer on the same day that I was diagnosed. Kelley was in her early thirties, with a young preschooler and an infant. I was lucky to have older children. I also realized that when someone was diagnosed with breast cancer, I felt a bond with her.

I followed Kelley's story over the next few months and was amazed by her positive attitude and the necessary service she provided to the world by allowing us into her life and heart. She helped me through long days by validating my mixed-up feelings.

· well at least ·

I play a mind game with myself in order to put my life in perspective and time and time again, it works. This is how it goes: Say I'm in a car accident and my car is totaled. I think, *Well, at least I'm okay and no one got hurt.* Or I have a really stressful day at work and think, *Well, at least I'm lucky to have a job.*

I continued this game after being diagnosed. *Well, at least I was diagnosed and not one of my kids. Well, at least it hasn't spread anywhere else. Well, at least I can finish my master's program.* There is always something worse than the situation I'm in.

I went to the hospital to have my sentinel node biopsied to see if any lymph nodes were involved in addition to my breast cancer. While I was waiting for my husband to bring the car around to pick me up so I could go home, there was a woman in a wheel chair who wasn't able to walk. I thought, *Well, at least I can walk to the car!*

· windex ·

*T*he day prior to having sentinel node surgery, I went to the hospital to have my breast injected with dye. The purpose of this process is to let

the breast drain the dye into the sentinel node. If other nodes besides the sentinel node end up blue, those nodes are also removed and biopsied.

The surgery went fine, but I was surprised that my urine was Windex blue when I got home. I called my daughter in to the bathroom to see how crazy it looked! My brother-in-law thought it was weird that I showed Kenzie, but my sister Linda and I laughed!

· lunch break ·

The day after the surgery, my sisters and mother came over for lunch. I felt pretty well, but I was tired and had an appointment with the medical oncologist that afternoon.

I met with the oncologist later that day and she decided to start my first chemotherapy treatment that Friday. I was surprised that I would start so soon, but figured that the sooner I started, the sooner I would get it behind me.

I spoke to my sister Linda after my appointment, and she told me she wasn't ready to have me start chemo. I didn't feel very ready either.

· e-mail ·

I e-mailed everyone after a big appointment because it was exhausting to go to the appointment, absorb all of the information, and then relay that information to everyone. I also didn't think it was fair to be on the phone during dinner and have the kids hear me retell the news.

Everyone understood this mode of communication. I saved the e-mails that I got in return; they were funny, sad, and uplifting.

· jane ·

$\mathcal{M}$y husband Brian must have looked pretty distracted at work, because one of the nurses that he worked with asked him if everything was okay. He was tired, worried, and possibly wondering who would clean those damn bathrooms if something happened to me. Just kidding!

Jane gave to us unquestioning and constant support over the months that followed. She is a ten-year breast cancer survivor, which offered me hope.

When Brian would come home from work, I'd ask if he spoke to Jane that day. Most days, Jane offered information, hope, or relief from the confusion that surrounded us and filled our days. Jane fought her breast cancer as a single mother of two small children.

I never met Jane, but she helped Brian and me through this trying time in our lives more than she will ever know. I hope our paths cross someday.

· classmates ·

I had been studying for my Master's degree for a couple of years and was finally going to graduate in the spring. My classmates and I had been through pretty crazy times with difficult classes and trying to manage our schoolwork, jobs, and families. We were a pretty close-knit group. Our professor was very sweet.

When class was almost over, our professor asked if anyone had any questions. This was my moment to tell my news. I would have never told them if it weren't for the fact that my hair would be falling out in a couple of weeks and I'd be donning a wig.

I told them and they offered their support with schoolwork if I needed it. They remained supportive throughout the semester. They made the semester tolerable.

In my other class, I only knew Sue. I told her and the professor my news. I didn't think it necessary to tell people just for the sake of it. I only missed one class out of twenty-eight during that semester. I emailed the professor the day I missed class and said that I wouldn't be in that evening. He emailed me back, "Understood." He never mentioned it again. I was grateful for his understanding.

Sue was a bright point during my treatment. She stopped in to every chemo treatment to say hello and she always brought me something. I looked forward to our visits and she made the time go by so much quicker. We always had a few laughs.

· first chemo treatment ·

I have been a nurse for over twenty years and have seen and heard just about everything . I have seen families given poor prognoses from physicians and I never really gave much thought to the word oncology or oncologist. But I suddenly found myself a patient in the oncology unit with my own oncologist. It was very unnerving to be a full-fledged member of the cancer center.

Brian accompanied me to my first chemo. We decided that he would accompany me to my first chemo treatment and then my brother, sisters, and mother would come to the other seven sessions. Brian had missed a fair amount of work coming to my many appointments. Everyone kept asking what they could do for me. I didn't need anything, but if they could keep me company during my several-hour treatments, the time would go by more quickly.

I registered at the front desk of the cancer center then rounded the corner to have my weight and vital signs taken. I didn't need to have my blood drawn for this appointment because it had been drawn a couple of weeks prior. My next stop was the infusion center. I looked up and saw the mom of one of Travis' friends standing there in her scrubs. I knew she was a nurse, but didn't know she was a nurse in this particular clinic. I hugged her and told her how happy I was to see her. She said she was not happy to see me there.

Beth made all of my chemo treatments easier. She was funny and knowledgeable, and I looked forward to seeing her. If she happened to have a day off, she had someone else keep an eye out for me. I, in turn, brought her bagels and tried to be a good patient.

· catheter ·

I didn't need a special intravenous line or catheter . I was glad for that, and didn't mind having an IV put in every two weeks for chemo. I figured I would feel less sick and wouldn't have the reminder because the line would be removed after every treatment.

Beth gave me IV medications to prevent nausea. Prior to arriving that morning, I took other anti-nausea meds. I had several prescriptions and kept the bottles in a plastic container for the few days that I needed them, but the minute I didn't need them, the container was tucked away until the next treatment. I hated taking the meds, but I was grateful to have them, because I had seen so many patients become terribly ill as a side effect of chemo before such meds were available.

The next step was IV Adriamycin pushed directly into my vein. I was very calm. The Adriamycin was pinkish red like Kool-Aid and I can promise you that I will *never* drink anything that resembles Kool-Aid again.

Next was Cytoxan. I printed all of the information about the chemo drugs and read the side effects. I then decided to throw away all the information. As I read the side effects and worried, I was afraid I would never sleep again! The Cytoxan took only about ninety minutes to go in. When the treatment was over, I drove myself home.

· gail ·

I had many appointments during each week. Gail was one of the secretaries who booked appointments as well as registered patients for appointments. She was so pleasant in spite of being so busy.

Sometimes she needed to change the schedule around to accommodate an early appointment for my chemo. She told me that she would call me with the new time, and she always called back when she said. I loved her smile and ability to stay cool on the busiest of days. People like Gail made the ordeal bearable.

· is bald really beautiful? ·

I have never been too concerned about my hair. Suddenly, it was important to me to have hair. I wondered if I might not lose it, but Beth brought me back to reality when she said that some people believed that their hair wouldn't fall out. I never confessed that I was one of those believers.

My hair was due to fall out about two weeks after my first treatment. Apparently, my eyebrows could be spared, but would probably get thin. My eyebrows are very dark, like caterpillars. I couldn't imagine not having them.

It remained part of my daily routine to wash my head with shampoo even though my hair was gone. I longed for normalcy in this new chapter of my life.

· cement ·

I was told that chemo would cause constipation, but never expected how severe it could be. It was like I poured a fresh bag of cement into a bowl, mixed it with the perfect amount of water, grabbed myself a big spoon, devoured the entire bowl, and waited for it to harden.

One day I was in agony and I *almost* called my brother-in-law, who worked nearby, and my mother-in-law, who lived nearby to come over. I'm not quite sure what I would have said or done once they got here, but the constipation was an experience I hope to never endure again. Thankfully, I never did call.

· new-nasty ·

Thursday was my chemo day, but I always felt great on Friday. My husband gave me the prescribed shot of Neulasta the day after each chemo treatment. It stung at first. The following day, my joints ached and I sweat like crazy all night long. I hated the Neulasta more than the chemo, but again, I was grateful to have it.

The Neulasta stopped my white blood cell count from falling dangerously low because of the chemo and lessened the chance of infection. I wished this medication had been available when my dad was sick, because it may have stopped the many infections he battled over the years.

When I next saw my oncologist, she said an older patient in her practice named it *New-nasty* and refused to take it. I think she was brave to decline this medicine, but I was afraid not to take it!

I continued to hate Neulasta, but tried to keep its effects in perspective.

· incoming ·

*C*ards, gifts, flowers, and meals started arriving. They carried notes of encouragement and statements saying that if anyone could beat this, I could. I was always grateful that someone was thinking of me, and I learned that people kept me in their prayers. I don't consider myself to be especially religious (more spiritual), but I truly appreciated the prayers.

One of my favorite gifts was a "Jack's Pack." It was a hatbox of goodies that my sister's friend Jen made in memory of her dad Jack. In the hat box was an assortment of carefully thought out personal items that had brought comfort to Jen's dad during his chemo treatment.

I loved the hatbox and kept my get-well cards in it. Jen was fascinated by my story and thought that my family was a bit offbeat with our humor regarding my diagnosis. I find humor an amazing stress buster and can find something funny about most situations. This was no exception.

Jen checked on me through my sister Linda and was a great support to her throughout my ordeal. When I met her, she encouraged me to write down my thoughts and my experience because I had such a funny outlook. She assured me that I would be on *Oprah* someday. I was not so sure about that.

My sister, Karen, and her husband dropped over with dinner and a gift. Dinner was a prime rib with mashed potatoes, gravy, and carrots. It was delicious! It was one of the best dinners I have ever had. I also got a pair of pajamas that were beyond comfortable.

· cancer is so limited... ·

It cannot cripple LOVE.
It cannot shatter HOPE.
It cannot corrode FAITH.
It cannot destroy PEACE.
It cannot kill FRIENDSHIP.
It cannot suppress MEMORIES.
It cannot silence COURAGE.
It cannot invade the SOUL.
It cannot steal eternal LIFE.
It cannot conquer the SPIRIT.

—AUTHOR UNKNOWN

· basketball ·

Kenzie decided to play sixth-grade basketball and her friends re-cruited her to play on their team. Although she had never played before, she was a pretty good athlete. I was happy that she would play, but wasn't sure what to expect with my treatment, so I hesitated to let her sign up. Kenzie asked me if I could pick up her friend Shannon, who had lost her mother just a few months before basketball started. Shannon is a great friend to Kenzie, and I was happy to help her out with a ride every week.

Basketball was a great diversion, and Kenzie and her team made a lot of progress over the course of the season. Kenzie got pretty good at handling the ball, but her shooting skills were pretty horrific. She threw these absolute bombs toward the hoop. Amazingly, some shots went in, but many didn't. Her games were on Sundays but during chemo, I felt pretty lousy by that day. I made it to most games and thoroughly enjoyed the distraction.

· lilly ·

*W*hen I first graduated from nursing school in 1986, I got a job on a medical-surgical unit in a local hospital. The unit next to me also had some new grads and one of them was Lilly. I was instantly drawn to her. We worked alongside each other for many years, and would sometimes head out after a long evening shift for a quick beer before heading home.

We got married around the same time and had kids close to one another. We had lost touch over the last few years, but we always asked about each other if we met a mutual acquaintance and always sent Christmas cards to each other.

Lilly was one of the first people to send a card. In it, she said that her doctor had found a lump in her armpit and she was concerned. I hoped for the best but Lilly was also diagnosed with breast cancer.

We shared a lot of cards, poems, and logged some phone time over the next few months. I was sorry about her diagnosis, but was happy that I could share this process with someone whom I cared about so much. We said we couldn't wait to look back and have all of this behind us, but knew that we had an awful lot ahead.

· hair today, gone tomorrow ·

*E*xactly two weeks after my first chemo treatment, my hair started to fall out. I had so much thick hair and I was surprised that it didn't come out in clumps. It came out in layers, and it was everywhere. I couldn't believe that it was going to fall out. I put on a baseball hat (from my Jack's Pack), but even with the hat, it continued to fall out. After a few days, I couldn't stand the hair being everywhere.

I had planned on having my husband shave my head on Sunday, but I couldn't stand it one more day. When I took a shower, I decided to see how much of my hair would come out if I tugged on it. The noise that it made when I tugged on it made me sick to my stomach. It was loud (at least to me), like something ripping. Brian was in the bathroom at the time and heard the noise. My hair and tears filled up the shower and there was nothing I could do about either one.

After some coaxing, we stayed in the bathroom to buzz my head with the same clippers that had buzzed the boys' heads for so many summers. I still had a lot of hair left, but the fact that it was coming out so slowly made me crazy.

Brian started to cry, and I kept saying that it was okay, *Just buzz it!* When he was finished, Kenzie walked into the bathroom and said, "Hey Mom, that's not so bad!" I knew right then that I was going to keep her.

· attitude ·

I emailed this to my friends and family when my hair fell out. I thought it might make them feel a bit better.

ATTITUDE

There once was a woman who woke up one morning, looked in the mirror, and noticed she had only three hairs on her head.

"Well," she said, "I think I'll braid my hair today." So she did and she had a wonderful day.

The next day she woke up, looked in the mirror and saw that she had only two hairs on her head. "Hmm," she said, "I think I'll part my hair down the middle today. So she did and she had a grand day.

The next day she woke up, looked in the mirror, and noticed that she had only one hair on her head. "Well," she said, "Today I'm going to wear my hair in a pony tail." So she did and she had her best day, so far!

The next day she woke up, looked in the mirror, and

noticed that there wasn't a single hair on her head. "Yahoo!" she exclaimed, "I don't have to fix my hair today!"

Bottom Line: Attitude is everything. As the saying goes: "The kind of life you will have isn't determined by what happens to you, it's determined by your reaction to what happens to you."

Have a great day.

—AUTHOR UNKNOWN

· debut ·

The following day, Kenzie had a basketball game, and my sister was going to come and watch it with her four children. We got about half-way through the game when I got up the courage to ask her what she thought about my wig. "Your wig?" she said. "I didn't even notice you had it on. I thought you were going to shave your head tomorrow."

My wig and I spent a lot of time together after that day. I hated the thought of it, but was happy to have it, though there were several draw-backs to it. If the wind blew, the sides of the wig blew up and revealed the bald sides of my head. I hated the wind from that moment on. The other drawback was that my head got warm underneath the wig. *Well, at least it's winter!* I thought. I joked that wearing my wig was like wearing a dead raccoon on my head. I hated that raccoon, but had a lot of respect for women who forego the wig and wear a turban or bandana. An awful lot of respect.

I didn't wear my wig around the house. I wore a hat or nothing at all. I was amazed at how the kids didn't flinch if they ate dinner with their bald mother.

· locks of love ·

I was volunteering at the concession stand during Kenzie's basketball game one afternoon and I noticed that the sister of one of Kenzie's teammates had a new haircut. She told me that she had cut her long hair and donated the ponytail to Locks of Love so someone who may need a wig could have one. I told her and her mom that she had done a wonderful thing. It was a selfless act for such a young girl.

There I was with my new wig, feeling very self-conscious but pretending everything was normal. Her desire to help others made my day. Abbey is well beyond her years and is one of my favorite people.

· cravings ·

The chemo didn't make me sick, but it was like being pregnant. I had to eat several small meals a day in order to ward off nausea. Even though I took the anti-nausea drugs, I had a few sick waves.

I craved iced tea and McDonald's vanilla shakes. The last time I had a shake from McDonalds was about thirty years ago. I also craved Pepsi. I craved Cheez-It crackers, another food I hadn't eaten in a long time. Scrambled eggs always tasted good to me. Every day before lunch, I thought about a turkey and provolone sandwich.

One morning after grocery shopping, I wanted maple walnut ice cream. It was 9 o'clock in the morning when I marched into a local restaurant in search of a scoop of ice cream. I ate it in the car before heading home.

Another day, as I was eating a bowl of Cheerios, I realized that they tasted just like lobster. Brian said that next time we went to Maine for lobster, we could bring some Cheerios for me. I'd be a cheap date.

· jim ·

My sons have friends who are brothers. A few weeks before I was diagnosed, their mother died of inflammatory breast cancer, a difficult cancer to treat. Her husband, Jim, was grocery shopping in the store where Travis works and made a point to tell Travis that his wife's cancer was very different from the cancer I had. He told Travis that I would be okay, and not to compare the two of us. It meant a lot to me and to Travis to hear this from Jim.

· smile anyway ·

My new motto was *smile anyway*. No matter how I felt, it made me happier to smile. I believe that it made those around me happier if I tried not to dwell on my condition and instead made our lives as normal as possible.

Brian thought we should make T-shirts with this motto on them. I think everyone should adopt this type of positive attitude. The world may be a bit brighter.

· osama and britney ·

*n*ow that I was a bald woman, I drove my husband crazy. I thought of the worst people who ever lived and wondered why they deserved to have hair. My conversations were one sided: "Saddam Hussein had hair. Osama bin Laden has hair. Why did Hitler get to have hair, if I can't?"

Britney Spears shaved her head after a mental breakdown. I couldn't imagine doing that, nor did I have the means to get hair extensions or stunning wigs. I had a much nicer shaped head than she did, and my ears were cuter.

· does anybody really know ·
what time it is?

I took my watch off. My life with cancer was unfamiliar to me. Before, I worked, studied for my Master's degree, and did clinical hours. Suddenly, I wasn't working for the *first time* in twenty years. I have always had tons of energy, and I just didn't have it anymore. My life consisted of multiple doctors' appointments, so I decided I didn't need my watch.

Before my diagnosis, time was precious, and I had limited time to accomplish a lot of things. Since I had been diagnosed, time was more precious, but it went by more slowly. I put my watch away and didn't put it back on for months. I went from wearing it twenty-four hours a day to not needing it. I didn't recognize the person I had become, and I didn't like being this tired person at all.

· valentine ·

My mother, sisters, and brother created a Valentine basket of treats for me: wonderful chocolates, lotions, books, teas, and a gift certificate for a local spa. It was so nice to have all of my favorite things in one basket. I decided that a pedicure was in order.

I made an appointment and looked forward to being pampered. I arrived at the spa and was ready for the pedicure when a little boy ran over and started playing in the water that my feet were in. He splashed, yelled, and truly disrupted any sense of relaxation. On my way home, I became aggravated that I wasn't able to enjoy a few minutes of pampering. My sisters and I laughed about it later.

· only one girl ·

During my treatment, one of my favorite sayings was, "I'm only one girl." I had created and adopted this motto long before breast cancer was part of my life. I worked tirelessly from sunup to sundown every-day. *But I was only one girl.* I could only do so much! Although it helped me before my diagnosis, it really hit home during treatment.

· dinner ·

I had to cancel dinner plans with some high school buddies when I was first diagnosed. I would have been lousy company, in spite of my "smile anyway" motto. We rescheduled after my first chemo treatment. I felt really good that night and was happy to be distracted for a while. I hadn't had anything alcoholic to drink, and was not supposed to according to the doctor because of the chemo and my poor liver. I drank a half a glass of wine that night. It tasted wonderful.

We had dinner and laughed about the crazy things we did in high school and caught up with what was going on in our lives at that time. The night ended much too quickly, and we promised to get together once my hair grew back.

Cheryl stopped me in the parking lot and asked if I wanted to join her and her sister in a breast cancer walk in the spring. I was honored that she and her sister wanted to walk for me and all of those affected by this type of cancer. I was afraid to commit, because I never knew how I was going to feel. I hated not being able to make plans. I truly hated it. And to be honest, living in the moment was aggravating, too. I knew that the inability to make plans would be temporary, but I went from being an energetic person to a zero energy person.

We decided to participate in a walk at a later time. I am looking forward to it.

· rumors ·

I had worked in a hospital for nearly twenty years, and decided to take a leave of absence because of my diagnosis. I didn't want to commit to work when I didn't know if I would be able to work my scheduled twelve-hour shifts. I had heard through a hospital rumor that I had a poor prognosis. I was infuriated that people who knew nothing about my story were spreading misinformation. I realized how damaging words could be.

On the other hand, my friends protected me. They spread positive news and kept information from those who were nosey. I never asked my friends to do this, but was grateful for their respect for my privacy.

· round two ·

*B*y the time I started to feel like myself again, it was time for the second treatment. It was worse this time because I knew what was ahead of me. For this round, the chemotherapy was the same and I spent about four hours at the chemo infusion center. My brother Joe met me there to keep me company. He is one year older than me and is, without question, the best brother a girl could ask for. He tolerated the torment of four sisters.

Before I left that morning for the hospital, I listened to the Rodney Atkins song, "If You're Going Through Hell." It made me smile and for each chemo treatment after that, I played it a couple of times before I left the house. Winston Churchill originally said, "If you are going through hell, keep going."

Twenty-something years ago, my brother dropped off a huge brown teddy bear to my nursing school dorm for my birthday. Shortly before starting the second round of chemo, I came across it when cleaning out Kenzie's closet. I pulled the teddy bear down into my bedroom. It was my lucky charm.

Chemo went well, and my brother was exceptional chemo company. We had a chance to catch up and had a great time making the session go by. At one point, Joe took a walk and ran into the doctor for whom the cancer center was named. He gave my brother hope that breast cancer was a fairly easy cancer to treat. They talked about me and about old cars.

My brother invited me out for lunch, and said we could go anywhere. I was hoping he'd buzz me up to Maine for a lobster at Barnacle Billy's. He laughed, and we ended up at a local Italian restaurant for an amazing buffet. Afterwards, as I headed home, I realized that I was a quarter of the way through chemo.

· running ·

Since the age of fourteen, running had been my way to relieve stress. So for the past twenty-seven years, I headed out for a run a couple times a week to clear my head. Running helped me get the hate out. Now, when I really needed to relieve stress, I couldn't fall back on running because my joints hurt so terribly from the chemo and Neulasta. There were days after my treatment that I had severe back and knee pain.

When I went to see the oncologist before my next treatment, she asked me if I was still exercising. I told her no. Surprised, she asked me why, and stated that I should be exercising. I responded, "Let's hit your back and knees with a baseball bat, and see if you feel like exercising." There was nothing I would have loved more than to feel like my old self. I didn't look or feel like myself, and I wasn't sure that I ever would.

Over the course of my years of running, I ran in many 5Ks and a couple of half marathons. In 2004, my sister Erin and I participated in a triathlon, an accomplishment that made us proud. We learned how to swim in order to compete, trained hard, and were able to finish in a fairly respectable time.

I must have had breast cancer then. Shortly after that competition, I had my first mammogram because of the palpated lump my gynecologist had found.

· breakfast circuit ·

*T*he phone started to ring. Friends and relatives wanted to visit. It made everyone feel better if they could just see me. I met everyone at restaurants for breakfast and lunch. I was getting spoiled. One day, my cousins, Lynn and Mary, picked me up and we headed to lunch. They are, without question, two of the funniest people on the planet. We had a great lunch and were able to catch up on our crazy families. It was a great time.

· chemo ass ·

I have always been known for having a bubble butt. Suddenly, my butt was gone. Disappeared and flat. I'm not sure how it happened, but my husband dubbed it "chemo ass." I never recalled seeing "chemo ass" listed as a potential side effect.

· green bananas ·

During the eighteen years that I have been married, I have probably been grocery shopping at least a thousand times. Lately though, I hated going up and down the aisles to fill the grocery cart with food that I would probably never eat.

On one such trip, I stopped at the produce section and contemplated whether to buy green or yellow bananas. If I bought green ones, I didn't know if I would feel well enough in a few days to eat them by the time they turned yellow. I put the yellow bunch in the cart to be sure I would have them if I needed them. I was so unsure of what the next day might bring, it was a gamble for me to buy the green bananas. That scared me.

· insurance ·

a nurse from my insurance company called after I was diagnosed to see if she could help me to get medications or scheduling appointments. She was a patient advocate. I remembered seeing a T.V. commercial during October. In the commercial, a young woman named Isabelle received a call from her insurance company. When the nurse Beth called (yes, another Beth!), I laughed and said, "I was waiting for you to call."

We talked for about forty-five minutes even though I didn't need her to advocate for me. I had received a lot of help squaring away my medications from Beth, the nurse at the oncology clinic. I spoke to Beth from the insurance company a couple of times. She was always upbeat and positive. I looked forward to her calls.

· round three ·

My younger sister Linda was my third-round chemo buddy. She was the one who would call me and ask me questions that no one else would ever think to ask. She thought she was bugging me, but I didn't mind at all. She kept good track of me. Three rounds down and five to go. My one-day-at-a-time theory was working out.

· sister study ·

*a*n article in one of the magazines in the waiting room was about a Sister Study for sisters of breast cancer patients. The study originated from the National Institute of Environmental Health, National Institute of Health, and the Department of Health and Human Services. It followed the participating sisters for several years and was very thorough in its assessment. I mailed each of my three sisters a copy, and said that if they had any interest in participating, that would be great. If not, no pressure.

Over the course of my diagnosis and treatment, no one ever asked me about my habits, risk factors (other than family history), or any environmental factors. I believed this was an omission, so I thought the Sister Study would trace the lives of my sisters and help to determine the cause of this disease.

My sister Karen did not join, and my sister Erin was too young according to the criteria. My sister Linda signed up and found it interesting. She filled out paperwork and had a visit from someone from the study. I was intrigued with this research. Those performing the study wanted to continue this research with the hope of including those diagnosed with breast cancer.

· comic relief ·

Tyler looks like me. Every once in a while, Ty took my wig, put it on his head, and danced around the house. He looked just like me! We cracked up. It was a great stress relief.

I look like my dad. When I looked at my bald self in the mirror, all I saw was my dad looking back.

I wanted to fight this battle with as much courage, dignity, and grace as he did.

· wig ·

You might have heard the old saying, "What do you have, a hair across your ass?" Well, one day, one of the kids was crabby, and I said, "What do you have, a wig across your ass?" We busted a gut!

Sometimes I thought maybe our humor was off. But a laugh could turn a bad day around better than most anything else.

· pay it forward ·

I had been working on a project in my class on family theory. The objective was to watch a movie and its family dynamics and apply a family theory to it. My group chose *Pay It Forward*. If you have never seen the movie, I urge you to watch it.

The premise is that if you do something nice for someone, they, in turn, do something nice for several people, the world will be a better place.

I had an appointment with my oncologist and was telling her about the hair stylist who recognized me from over twenty years ago. She said it's just like *Pay It Forward*. She had no idea that I had been heavily engrossed in studying the dynamics of the movie. It was a coincidence.

I have always liked poems or quotes that make me introspective. I saw the following piece when I was waiting for an appointment at the hospital one day.

ATTITUDE

The longer I live, the more I realize the impact of attitude on life.

Attitude, to me, is more important than facts. It is more important than the past, than education, than money, than circumstances, than failures, than successes, than what other people think or say or do. It is more important than appearance, giftedness, or skill. It will make or break a company...a church...a home.

The remarkable thing is we have a choice every day regarding the attitude we will embrace for that day. We cannot change our past. We cannot change the fact that people will act in a certain way. We cannot change the inevitable.

The only thing we can do is play on the one string we have, and that is our attitude...I am convinced that life is 10% what happens to me, and 90% how I react to it.

And so it is with you...we are in charge of our attitudes.

—CHARLES SWINDOLL

· chemo adventure ·

I could never predict how I would feel or what to expect. Chemo was an adventure every day. I became weary of the unpredictability of the symptoms and side effects, and decided that I was going to try to go along with it and hoped it would pass quickly.

· elizabeth edwards ·

*A*round this time, Elizabeth Edwards came forward and spoke about the fact that she now had cancer in her rib area. I applauded her courage to divulge this information and to be able to speak so eloquently about her treatment and prognosis. I also gave her a lot of credit, because she was not going to let her latest diagnosis interfere with her husband's dream to go to the White House.

There are approximately twelve million cancer survivors in this country who live productive lives. Elizabeth represented us well and put a human face to how well we survivors face the world and our responsibilities. Her untimely death was tragic, but her legacy continues.

· cd ·

I am a huge music fan and always find songs that help me through a difficult time. My sisters Linda and Erin sent me a CD called *Kick Cancer's Ass!* It included a compilation of tunes to let me know I was loved and to bring me strength. I loved to listen to the songs in the car.

One day I was riding on the back roads with the kids (we live on the edge of a huge state forest) and we were listening to a country radio station. A song called "Tough" by Craig Morgan came on the radio, about how tough the man thought he was until he saw his wife battle breast cancer. We were all choked up by the time the song finished. One of the boys said, "That song reminds me of you." Every time I hear that song, I still get choked up.

My sisters also sent Volume 2 of *Kick Cancer's Ass!* and I still listen to it every now and then.

· faucet ·

One symptom I had was a perpetually runny nose. I believe it was from the Adriamycin, because my friend Lilly had the same issue. I was on the phone one day with my sister Linda complaining about my perpetually running nose, when I realized that I had no nose hairs. We laughed. "No wonder your damn nose is running all the time," she said.

· vip status ·

*D*oors opened for me when I even breathed the word cancer. I had to order my Neulasta (New-nasty) from a pharmaceutical company each month, and they sent it by overnight delivery every two weeks. I was grateful to have insurance because the medication cost about $3,500 per dose.

The first time, I needed it to be delivered quickly because I started chemo sooner than I thought. Brian called the company and explained the situation. The woman on the other end was amazing and had it shipped so that I had it in time. Brian must have sounded stressed and tired to her.

Another time in CVS, I needed help with my prescriptions. The pharmacist stayed on the phone a long time with the insurance company while I waited for the medication to be clarified.

When I went into the pharmacy, I was treated like a celebrity. Everyone was extra nice. I thanked one of the pharmacists when my treatment was over because she was so patient with me.

During one of Kenzie's basketball practices, one of the other mothers brought me hot chocolate while we waited for the girls. Over those months, I was the recipient of many small acts of kindness and they always made me feel so good.

· the human furnace ·

*T*he combination of Neulasta and chemo caused serious hot flashes. I was a human furnace several times each day, and at night, I sweated like crazy and had to change my clothes. It made me tired to disrupt my much-needed sleep to cool off.

Another symptom was that I could feel every single lymph node in my chest and the back of my neck. There are lots of them. This discomfort lasted for a couple of days, along with the hot flashes, night sweats, and joint aches. By the time my next round of chemo came around, much of these effects diminished and it was time to get back on the chemo carousel.

· round four ·

*M*y treatment was coming to the halfway point and I couldn't have been happier. I knew what to expect from the meds and got pretty clever at managing my symptoms. My sister Erin accompanied me for number four. She was great company, even though she was many months pregnant.

The patient sitting next to me talked about getting a glass of wine after a nurse joked about passing a drink cart around. Erin said she'd make a run to the package store if he wanted. We joked about how our poor livers would fare if we drank alcohol *while* receiving chemo.

People were pretty upbeat while receiving their treatment, and I met a lot of nice people. I was amazed at how many young people were receiving treatment and saddened by those who were ill or by themselves during treatment.

· perspective ·

One day my sister Linda called and said that she wondered if we were giving my sister Erin enough attention regarding her pregnancy. I had woken up that morning with two chipped bottom teeth presumably from my grinding them because of stress.

I had tried very hard to keep track of everyone's lives. I made a huge effort to call Erin after her obstetric appointments, but I was in survival mode and I had all I could do to take care of myself.

It was a Monday and I hated those Mondays when I hadn't rebounded yet from chemo. To make matters worse, I couldn't get a dentist appointment for a couple of days and a snowstorm was brewing.

The next call of the day was from my mother. She told me that one of my sisters had a urinary tract infection. I thought to myself, *"What do you want me to do for her...make her supper or something?"*

My NSB Francie happened to call shortly after my sister and mother and I started to cry. She didn't know what to do with my tears, so she put one of her co-workers on the phone who had survived cancer. After a pretty impressive pep talk from her co-worker, I felt a little better.

I finally made it to the dentist a couple of days later and had my teeth bonded. The dentist was great and has been my dentist for twenty some-

thing years. His hygienist was also very sweet. Her brother had been battling pancreatic cancer and she gave me a pink ribbon and told me that
she would pray for me.

· even the strong can break ·

*T*he good news is that I am not a very vain person. The bad news is that I was having trouble with my self-image. Not only was I bald, my fingertips ached and my fingernails looked strange. I had half moon–shaped rings on my nails starting at my cuticles. The oncologist said that some people develop a "ring" for each chemo treatment they receive.

I had seen on T.V. that a women's college basketball coach wore band-aids where her fingernails had been. They had fallen out because of the medication that she took for her breast cancer, and her fingertips were very painful. I gave her a lot of credit for continuing to coach, because it was her passion. I thought, *Well, at least I have my fingernails.*

· round five ·

I was going to start my fifth chemo treatment and just as I had gotten used to the side effects, my chemo medication was going to change to Taxol for the next four treatments. I would probably have fewer gastrointestinal side effects. This infusion of Taxol would take a bit longer to administer than the previous type of medication. The medication would be administered through a slow drip to be sure I didn't have a reaction. All went as planned. Brian came with me, because it was a new medication. I went home and couldn't believe that I only had three more rounds to go. Time flies when you're having fun.

The Sunday night after I received the first dose of Taxol, I woke up in the middle of the night in excruciating pain. I have always thought that I have a very high tolerance for pain, but I was in agony. Not only did I have the usual joint pain and lymph node pain, I also had sharp, shooting, sit-up-straight-in-the-bed pain in my left breast. I slept very little that night. I was tired, scared, and sick of the whole ordeal.

By morning, I felt a little better, but I was exhausted. My oldest sister Karen said that The Fucker must have self-destructed during the night. I sure hoped so. I needed some positive news.

· on fire ·

a couple of days later, I had more severe, dripping night sweats. It was scary to see and feel the beads of sweat form on my skin. I improvised a bit at night and put a beach towel on top of my sheets. During the night, I tossed the drenched towel off the bed, pulled a pair of dry pajamas out from under my pillow, changed into them, flipped my pillow over, and went back to sleep.

When I developed a fever and cough, it was time to call the doctor. I couldn't reach the oncologist, so I called my primary doctor who told me to come right in. He drew blood, gave me antibiotics, and I headed home. In the meantime, I heard from my oncologist and they wanted to see me the next day.

· the third beth ·

I headed into the oncologist's office the next day and saw Beth the nurse practitioner. Beth was always someone I was happy to see. She has a very calming way about her and she had worked with Brian almost twenty years before. She was also the third Beth that I had come in contact with over the last couple of months.

Beth checked me out and I asked her if they were trying to kill me with the last round of chemo. She didn't realize that I was joking (kind of) and proceeded to tell me that I had a toxic reaction to the Taxol and the dose of the next cycle would be reduced. I also got a shot of Procrit, because I had become anemic during the course of the treatment. I had been more tired than usual and was glad to have the Procrit every couple of weeks if I needed it to boost my counts.

I was also too sick to get chemo that week, so I made an appointment for the following week. I thought that a setback or delay in getting treatment would bother me, but as my brother Joe said, I had actually gained a week because they had started my chemo so quickly.

· dying ·

I was still feeling pretty fearless, in spite of my being sick over those few days. I didn't realize how sick I actually was until I started to feel better. Once I had more energy and my fever was gone and my white count was normal, my cough disappeared and the sweats subsided to their usual level of aggravation.

It was around this time that I realized that I wasn't afraid of dying. It certainly wasn't an option for me, but there were some days when I was so sick that if I had fallen asleep and not woken up, it wouldn't have been the worst thing in the world to me. I had *so much* to live for and look forward to that I never hoped I *wouldn't* wake up; it just wouldn't have been the worst thing in the world.

· grocery shopping ·

*B*rian offered to go to the grocery store because I was still pretty wiped out. In the nearly two decades that we had been married, Brian probably had gone to the grocery store only once or twice.

I wondered what he was thinking when going to the grocery store was now on his radar. I was grateful for his help. If only I could get him to clean those bathrooms.

· good health ·

It's amazing what prompts us to think of things.

When I was at my wedding shower, my Great Aunt Julia (we called her Jimmie) pulled me aside and said that she wished me a long, happy, and healthy life. I remember thinking that this was a silly thing to say to me. After all, I was a perfectly healthy bride-to-be at twenty-two years old and couldn't even fathom being otherwise. I hadn't thought of this in years.

· blue-light special ·

I really wanted a new refrigerator. I couldn't stand my old fridge, and, after some persuasion, I talked Brian into letting me buy a new one.

It was a mild day in March as I made my way to the appliance store. I felt good and had the radio blaring a Sheryl Crow song that I was singing along to, when all of a sudden, I saw blue police lights flashing. I couldn't believe it. I was being pulled over for speeding! The officer read me the riot act, and I considered telling him that I was just getting out of the house after being sick and snowed in, but I didn't. He let me go with a warning, and I managed to find another great tune to belt out, only this time, I drove a little more slowly as I sang.

· class work ·

I rebounded pretty well, but had some intense class work to deal with. I was given my written comprehensive exam in the middle of March. This is how it went: I had to choose two topics out of five and write a ten-page paper for each chosen topic within two weeks. The assignment involved research and lots of work preparing two quality essays.

At the same time, Mackenzie was leaving for Florida with my mother-in-law, sister-in-laws, and her cousins. I had to shop for her Florida clothes, pack her up, and send her off.

Simultaneously, Brian and the boys were going ice fishing in Vermont for the long weekend. They had asked if I wanted them to stay home, but I thought that if I had the whole house to myself for the weekend, I could bang out these two papers with little difficulty.

· home alone ·

I can't recall the last time that I was home by myself for any length of time. I ran to the store and bought myself a steak, a potato, a summer squash, and prepared dinner for myself. A snowstorm was on its way, so I got out for a bit before I got snowed in.

After dinner, I started in on the papers. I love to write, and have always enjoyed school. I know, I'm a freak.

By the next morning, I was about halfway into my first paper and the snow was really falling outside. Brian's cousin tried to plow my car out, but his Jeep kept getting stuck and half of the driveway remained covered with snow. I wouldn't be able to get out, which actually gave me more incentive to get the papers written.

As I was typing away and feeling pretty damn good about how much I had accomplished, I accidentally hit a button on my laptop and lost the entire paper. I never thought to save it because no one was home to bother my laptop or move any of my research books. I couldn't believe it. I tried everything to get it back. I called my sister Erin, and she tried feverishly to help me. I panicked and called Travis in Vermont where he was ice fishing to see if he knew of a magic button that would return my work to my computer screen. Hell, I even called customer service at Dell to see what I could possibly do.

Then, I started to cry. By crying, I don't mean your run-of-the-mill crying, I blubbered and sniffled and sobbed. I'm not sure if I was crying because of the lost paper or because I was so tired of not being myself. I think that I cried more that afternoon than I had cried in all of my forty-two years combined. Brian even offered to come home from Vermont, but I said no. Now I really had some work to do.

· let it snow ·

I had to make up the five or six hours of lost work. I was also supposed to attend a birthday party that evening which was a couple of hours away.

I debated calling my sister Karen to tell her and her husband not pick me up for my aunt's surprise 70th birthday party. My driveway was a nightmare because of the snow, and I was in a foul mood because of the paper debacle.

I decided to take a shower, adjust my wig, and get over myself. I was ready to go when my sister drove up the driveway and proceeded to get her car stuck in a snow bank. It took nearly an hour to get it out before we headed out to meet the rest of my family.

Our next stop was my sister Linda's house, where we hopped into her Suburban and went to my cousin's for the party.

We were a motley crew: my mother, *very* pregnant sister, Erin, brother-in-law, Karen, and Linda. We arrived at the party and had a great time. I had some reservations about going. I really started to hate being the elephant in the room everywhere I went. My cousins and aunt, however, were very gracious and we had a wonderful evening.

As we made our way home, I was grateful that I hadn't let my lost paper ruin a visit with my family. But now I really had some catching up to do.

· milestone ·

I passed my papers in on time, successfully defended them, and finally realized that I would be able to graduate in May. I had been going to school for many years toward this goal and was pretty damn proud of myself. Maybe there was an end in sight. Graduation Day was on Mother's Day.

· new and improved ·

I have always hated driving in the car with my windows rolled down while my hair flew around. Suddenly I was a changed woman. I loved the windows rolled down with my wig hair flying in the breeze!

· courage ·

"Courage doesn't always roar. Sometimes courage is the quiet voice at the end of the day saying, 'I will try again tomorrow.'"

—MARY ANNE RADMACHER

· saving the world ·

I always thought that it would be wonderful to be a stay-at-home mom. I began to realize that my kids were busier than they had ever been before. I envisioned accomplishing incredible things if I wasn't bogged down by work. Oh, the time I would have to do all of the things I never seemed to have the energy to do! But, I missed the organized chaos of my life. I loved my too-full-of-commitments days.

While I was home for these months, I did very little to make the world a better place, although I did manage to start a recycling effort in the house (that was slowly bought into by the kids) and I did bring my old eyeglasses to the Lion's Club box in the post-office. But it didn't promote world peace, and then I realized that my role in this world was to bring up my kids to the best of my ability and to take care of patients as if they were my own family members.

It may not be much, but there is a small, bright, unwavering light coming from my little corner of the world. And somehow, that's enough for me.

· chemo brain ·

*I*n my practice as a nurse, I always wondered if chemo brain was a true phenomenon or not. But I can speak from experience that there is some truth that a brain that has indirectly received chemo is a brain that is slow to pull a word out, and finds it difficult to read and concentrate.

Some days, my chemo brain was a blessing. Other days, it was a curse. This phenomenon would lessen somewhat a few days after chemo finished, and I wondered if it was the anti-nausea medications that helped produced the fog.

Regardless, I hoped it was not a long-lasting side effect. Thankfully, my quick wit and words returned, but the fog lingered for a long time.

· shauna ·

I decided to treat myself to a pedicure. All the money I saved from missing a few months of haircuts could be put to good use. I needed a little pick-me-up anyway.

There is a spa near my home that is run by a very energetic and bright woman named Shauna. She is funny and outgoing and one of those people that you feel like you have known forever, even after a few minutes.

I walked in and was surprised to see her wearing a bandana with no visible hair underneath! My heart broke! She had been diagnosed with breast cancer a couple of months after I was, and she was a bit behind me with the chemotherapy.

We shared good stories, and she still had her sense of humor and lots of life in her beautiful eyes. I was envious that she wore a bandana and didn't care who stared at her. She challenged her husband to walk into Target with her one day because he didn't believe that people would stop and stare. Boy, was he surprised when he realized how blatant people were.

I preferred being incognito with my wig on. I soon realized that most people who were employed in malls or stores didn't even look up at me as I checked out. While I would have found that behavior rude a couple of months before, I welcomed their disinterest in me. Shauna was a great inspiration.

· menopause: to be or not to be ·

*T*he doctors were unsure whether I would ever get my period again. They claimed that if I was diagnosed with breast cancer at the age of thirty, it was pretty much guaranteed that I would get it back. If I had been fifty, it probably wouldn't return.

But because I was the very special age of forty-one, no one really knew. Part of me was thrilled that I would never get my period again...another part of me worried about my heart health and bone strength when I was eighty.

· spring is in the air ·

As spring arrived, Kenzie started softball and Ty played junior varsity baseball. Travis ran track for the high school. Everyone was in full swing.

One day, Kenzie pitched for her team during a game and had a little difficulty. One of the mothers remarked that Kenzie should really go and see a pitching coach to help her with her form. I had been paying attention to Kenzie's pitching and realized that her steps were off, which was making her pitch off balance.

When I told Kenzie, she quickly fixed her pitches. As for the mother, I wanted to scream at the top of my lungs that after the stressful winter my family had been through, the fact that she was on the pitcher's mound with a huge smile on her face was way more important than her strike count.

During one of Tyler's games, I was sitting in my chair during what appeared to be a small monsoon. My wig flopped around like puppy ears and I had to sit in the car to get out of the wind, adjust my wig, and regroup.

· round six ·

*M*y sister Linda met me for treatment number six. She is my next youngest sister. It is rare for me to have a several hour uninterrupted visit with a sibling. Even though the chemo days were long, the time I spent with my family was priceless.

Linda is the mother of four, with a set of twins. Christina and Danielle had heard my sister talking on the phone so many times about breast cancer and mammograms that they pretended to give mammograms to each other.

After my treatment, we left the hospital and headed out for pizza. I had forgotten to get money on my drive into the city that morning, so Linda graciously bought me lunch. Maybe the chemo brain was taking over; I think I still owe her for that lunch. Thankfully, this round of Taxol went much better than the first. My appetite and taste buds were almost back to normal. Cheerios tasted like Cheerios.

· tiny bubbles ·

I decided to take a long bath, hoping to alleviate some of my aches and pains. The basket full of goodies that my siblings and mother had given to me was going to come in handy. One of the goodies was bubble bath.

I poured some into the hot water, and immediately the bubbles rose out of the tub and poured out onto the floor. I called Brian and he helped me lift out armfuls of bubbles and put them into a nearby shower. We laughed as the bubbles kept coming and coming. Brian took my picture (I believe that this was the only picture of me with no hair). I did end up having a nice relaxing bath after that.

· round seven ·

y Mom, who had been hit pretty hard with my diagnosis, went with me to number seven. Sometimes, I got the sense that she did not think that I was going to do well. I'm sure she was thinking of my Dad when he had leukemia. One minute he was in remission, and within weeks, he was very sick again. Breast cancer is different. While I worried about the cancer spreading, my gut feeling was that I could beat it and live a long life.

My mother is silent in her support. She is a quiet woman compared to my boisterous self, but her quiet ways comfort me and she has always been a staunch supporter of me, even when I wore her out with my schemes and plans. For her, I am grateful.

· walking ·

By this time, I was actually able to get out and walk again, with minimal joint pain. After my initial reaction to the Taxol, I tolerated each treatment a bit better. It was wonderful to be out in the fresh air and exercising! I have always kept a log of my running and cross training. I was finally able to put entries into my log. It sure felt good.

· batting cages ·

I could not get over the fact that I might still need a mastectomy. I worried about this possibility for many, many months and still was terrorized by the thought. I also worried about lymphedema, which is swelling that can occur in a woman's arm following lymph node surgery. I had read that following breast or node surgery, women should be very careful about getting an infection in the affected arm. It is also important to not have blood drawn or blood pressure taken on the affected side.

I asked the oncologist about lymphedema. She believed that even though my risk may be minimal of developing lymphedema, I could be proactive. She suggested that I not lift more than ten pounds at a time. She also recommended wearing gloves while gardening or cleaning the house.

I asked a lot of questions about any limitations on physical activity that I may have. I loved to play softball with Kenzie and catch for her when she practiced pitching. I also loved to go to the batting cages at the beach with the kids. I was told these things would be fine.

· shopping ·

One of my favorite past times is shopping. I truly believe that I could shop every single day of my life.

I decided to stop into one of my favorite shops right in town; a shop full of antiques and primitives run by Kate. We have had many great conversations over the years, but I hadn't seen her since I was diagnosed and wasn't quite sure if the grapevine with my news had made it as far as Kate's shop. Apparently, it had not.

As I walked in she said, "I absolutely love your haircut!"

I didn't have the heart to tell her that it was the equivalent of a dead raccoon on my head. I'm not sure if she ever found out. I haven't been back yet.

· repeat mri ·

My next breast MRI was scheduled to be a few days before my last chemo. I was anxious to find out the results because those results would allow the surgeon to determine if I needed a mastectomy or a lumpectomy. The goal of having the chemotherapy first was to shrink the tumor so that it might be possible to have breast-conserving surgery. Waiting for the report from this test was excruciating.

· the grand finale ·

My last day of chemo was April 26th. Yes, I said my *last* day of chemo. I had made it through pretty much unscathed. I still had a lot ahead of me, but damn, I knew how much I had behind me! When someone would ask how chemo was, I'd say, "It wasn't too bad, but I wouldn't sign up for it again!"

I asked Beth if my results were back from the MRI. They weren't back yet. It was a Thursday, and I had to wait for the results through another weekend. The thought of waiting was unbearable.

The part that was bearable was that my sister Erin was in labor. We were both in the hospital and would each have a positive outcome. Erin called me mid-morning to tell me that her new son Martin Christopher was born. It was a great day. Martin was the little brother of seventeen-month-old Harry. The stars were aligned for a while, and I couldn't wait to meet Martin.

My day was also wonderful because all three of my NSBs came to my last chemo treatment with me. They had changed their work hours and met me first thing in the morning. Francie even picked me up at my house. I couldn't have been happier to have such great company. My only concern was that we would be laughing, and I was afraid of being disrespectful to those in the clinic who were not feeling so well.

When the last chemo infusion was complete, I walked out the door of the hospital and felt liberated. I truly believed that everything was going to be okay. We went out for pizza, and Francie and I headed out to meet baby Martin. Both Erin and Martin were doing well and her husband Chris was so proud of his beautiful family. He had a right to be.

· hope ·

My sister Karen called me to see if I had gotten my MRI results. I hadn't heard anything so Karen told me that they hadn't called because the doctors were running around the hospital with my films, showing everyone that The Fucker was gone! I laughed, knowing full well that I wasn't the luckiest girl on earth, and that this scenario would never happen.

· beth ·

On Friday, I stopped to send flowers to Beth, the infusion nurse who had taken such good care of me. They were to be delivered to her on Saturday.

In the middle of the afternoon on Saturday, Beth called me at home to thank me for the flowers. She also had the results of the MRI. She said the four sweetest words I have ever heard in my life. She told me the radiologist said there was *no evidence of malignancy*.

I couldn't fathom what she had said; I just couldn't fathom it. I was one of the lucky ones who had great results from the chemo. I asked what the results meant as far as surgery was concerned, and she understood that a lumpectomy was probably in my future because the surgeon would have to remove the marker and any dead tissue that may have been left behind. That sounded fine to me.

I had always thought that the sweetest four words ever spoken were when Brian told the kids, "Listen to your mother." I was wrong. "No evidence of malignancy" trumped everything!

When Brian walked in the door, and I told him the results of the MRI, his eyes filled up with tears. I took my first deep breath in months.

· call from mexico ·

My in-laws were on vacation in Mexico, and my mother-in-law called to check in. When I told her about my MRI results, she got choked up. It was so nice to have good news to share. My mother-in-law and sister-in-law made many meals during those long months of chemo and it was always so great to have a home-cooked meal for dinner.

· the eyes have it . . . or not! ·

*M*y eyelashes and eyebrows fell out. I made it to my very last treatment with four eyebrow hairs on my left eyebrow and only a couple more on my right side. I should have known when my eyebrows started to feel itchy. After that, my eyelashes fell out. I was highly insulted. I made it all the way through chemo and now had this to deal with! I was pretty crabby about it.

The hair on my head was just barely starting to come in like a shadow, and the hair on my legs also started to return. The break from shaving my legs had come to an end and I couldn't have been happier!

· honey brown ·

My friend Cathy (an NSB) called to tell me that her cousin had had chemo and had been afraid that when her hair grew back in, it would be gray. But she was thrilled when it grew back in a beautiful honey brown. I wasn't so lucky; freaking honey brown is not what grew in on *my* head. I had a salt and pepper nightmare going on. I must have said, "This isn't honey brown," at least a million times to Brian.

· interviews ·

I was due to graduate from the Master's program. My next mission was to land a job so I applied to a couple of local colleges with open faculty positions in their nursing programs. My first interview was two weeks after the chemo had ended. I bought myself a new suit, my sister Linda washed and styled my wig, and I was ready (somewhat) for my interview.

The morning I was getting ready for my interview, I looked in the mirror and was a bit horrified by my missing eyebrows and eyelashes. I had never envisioned myself interviewing for a job that I had worked so hard for looking like this. I told my husband that I looked like a freak from the circus and he said to stop bitching and get over myself. I refused to speak to him for several days.

I managed to get through the interview, and wasn't quite sure what to expect. I wasn't at the top of my game, but I had worked hard for a chance at the interview. Time would tell.

· penciled-in eyebrows ·

*T*he next interview was similar to the first. My eyebrows, or lack thereof, continued to haunt me, although I managed to put mascara on what may possibly have been the shortest eyelashes on any human being.

I arrived at the Human Resources Department and the man who greeted me had huge penciled-in eyebrows. I decided right then that the fact that he had fewer eyebrow hairs than I did was quite ironic. I laughed to myself. The interview went well with a panel of nursing professors. I felt pretty good as I left.

· near miss ·

aster's degree candidates dress in graduation caps and gowns and a colored hood is placed over their heads, which depicts their major. It was about 150 degrees in the auditorium and I had had a lot of hot flashes the previous night. I was also terrified that when the VP of the college put the hood over my cap, she would knock off both the cap and my wig. One of my classmates, Maureen, sat beside me and I told her my fear. She laughed and said it would never happen.

When it was my turn, I held my breath. The hood went on without a problem and I made it off the stage unscathed. A couple of students later, the VP did knock off a cap by mistake. Phew! I had dodged another bullet.

· phase two ·

I had an appointment with the surgeon, and she was amazed that there was no evidence of malignancy. My case was one of those discussed at a grand rounds meeting held by the oncology team. The decision was made that a lumpectomy would be the surgery of choice. The original date of my surgery was on Kenzie's twelfth birthday.

When the woman who booked the surgery called to confirm, I told her that it was Kenzie's birthday. I worried that if something went wrong, she would never forget that her birthday was a disaster. She rebooked it for the week following Kenzie's birthday without any hesitation.

· tan lines ·

As a long-time bikini wearer, and after seeing some pretty lousy lumpectomy scars, I decided that I was going to take matters into my own hands. I decided to lie out in the sun with my bikini top on and then ask or beg the surgeon not go beyond my bikini line when she operated if it was at all possible. It may sound crazy, but I think it helped me feel like I had some sense of control.

· surgery . . . again ·

he day of surgery, I arrived well before my scheduled time. I needed to have a needle localization done first. This meant that I had to have a needle inserted into where the marker was placed back when the entire process first began. The location of the needle was checked by a mammogram. I was lucky enough to have several mammograms that morning. Yes, I'm being facetious.

After that, I sat and waited with Brian. My brother-in-law and a friend work in the operating room where my surgery was scheduled to happen. They stopped in to say hello and to make the time go by. They set up a great nurse anesthetist whom I have known for a long time, to be with me during the case.

When the surgeon came in before surgery, I told her my bikini scheme. She said that she would try her best. Once surgery began, it went quickly. I remember talking towards the end of the surgery to the surgeon and I am not quite sure why she didn't tell me to stop talking. I went home the same day and felt pretty damn good.

· feeling groovy ·

*T*he day after the surgery, my sister Karen called to see how I was. I felt like a million bucks. I had no discomfort, and I met her at her friend's house for lunch. Phase two of my treatment was officially over.

· pathology report ·

My second interview at one of the colleges was two days after surgery. I donned my wig, drew on my eyebrows, and headed out the door to a beautiful day in May. My second interview was with the dean and a Vice President. It went well.

As I drove away from campus, my cell phone rang. It was the nurse practitioner who worked with the surgeon. She said that the pathology report was good and that I didn't need further surgery. Hopefully, my luck was changing. I sure hoped so.

· color my world ·

I ran to a CVS pharmacy to see about a rinse for my hair since honey brown didn't quite work out for me. I was debating what to do when a woman asked if she could help me. She introduced herself to me as the CVS color consultant. I told her that I had wanted to see about some color and told her about my wig. She asked if she could take a peak at my new hair under my wig. She proceeded to pick up the side of my wig to see what was underneath. I don't recall the rest of our conversation. I couldn't wait to get out of there to tell my sisters.

· butts ·

My sister Linda decided to host a girl's night. I headed over and we had fun. As I was leaving, my three sisters stood outside in the driveway, all smoking cigarettes. I was very angry. I told them that I must have made the entire chemo thing look way too easy if they could still contemplate smoking.

Later, Brian said that I should have thrown my wig on the ground and walked away for effect. I *wish* that I had thought of that.

· phase three: the final chapter ·

I healed very quickly and was dreading the weeks of radiation ahead. I met with the radiation oncologist, as she had been part of my original team that I had first met seven months ago. She was very kind, and I was very happy to see a familiar face. I figured that I would have this initial appointment and start the radiation the next day.

First, however, I was fitted for a mold that I would lie in to keep me still while I was in the radiation machine. I was also going to have my chest tattooed so that my chest and breast could be lined up with the machine to avoid any radiation from affecting areas other than my breast. I got very upset that I had to be tattooed.

I needed thirty-four radiation treatments. They were scheduled to start the day after the kids got out of school and continue Monday through Friday until the third week in August.

I was so tired of the entire breast cancer process. I wasn't sure I had it in me. I told Brian that I wasn't going to have the radiation treatments. I was sick of everything. I knew in my heart that I would never risk my health by not completing the prescribed treatment, but I had to think that I had some sort of clout for a while. I was so tired of it all.

· promise yourself ·

Promise yourself to be so strong that nothing can disturb your peace of mind.

Look at the sunny side of everything and make your optimism come true.

Think only of the best, work only for the best, and expect only the best.

Forget the mistakes of the past and press on to the greater achievements of the future.

Give so much time to the improvement of yourself that you have no time to criticize others.

Live in the faith that the whole world is on your side as long as you are true to the best that is in you.

—CHRISTIAN D. LARSON

· raccoon be gone ·

I ditched my wig finally and wore bandanas . . . very liberating. My hair was a crew cut, so I called myself Rapunzel.

My appointment in radiation oncology consisted of a mold made for me to lie in, pictures of my chest taken on a digital camera, and then I was tattooed. It was easy and involved three tiny, freckle-sized blue tattoos to my sternum, and under my breast with a small instrument. It was not worth shedding a single tear over. I was to start my radiation the following week.

· independence day ·

After a couple of weeks of radiation, the fourth of July was upon us. I decided to have my usual lobster cookout. My family came over and I figured that since it was Independence Day, my family was going to have to deal with me without my wig.

My sisters, except Linda, couldn't bear seeing me without my wig. I made it through most of the day, until Karen asked me to put my bandana back on. I was okay with that, after all, they hadn't seen me without my wig and I imagine it was a shock. I looked like a Chia Pet.

· the purple room ·

*R*adiation seemed to fly by. I met some really nice women who were also getting radiation, and we would chat in the purple waiting room. I loved my 8:15 a.m. appointment every day because I could get home just as the kids were getting up. The treatment itself only took about five minutes. It was painless.

One of the women there was kind to me, the newbie, saying that the machine would rotate over me and when the part of the machine that looked like a refrigerator came into view, the treatment was almost over. One of the other patients who lived in the next town over from me, said she never thought she'd have breast cancer at eighty. I replied that I never thought I'd be dealing with it at forty-one.

We became a pretty close group. We complained about everything from the stiff gowns to the misery of wishing our summer away, but at the same time, we were happy to be at the end of a long road. Some of the women became very tired from the radiation, but I felt fine. The women who worked in this department were as phenomenal as all the others that I had come in touch with. They were funny and personable and made me forget why I was there. We spent thirty-four summer mornings together.

· fishnet stockings ·

One of the radiation technicians told me about an elderly patient who had received radiation treatments several years before. She would put on a gown that only came to her waistline. Under the gown, she wore underpants, fishnet stockings and high heels.

When they told me the story, I envisioned a woman who didn't care what other people thought of her. She was going to be who she was. I was later told that the department invested in longer gowns.

· job offers ·

I was offered both jobs that I had applied for. I was back in the high life again. I accepted the one position, as a full-time nursing instructor, at the college where I had gone to graduate school, as I knew most of the people that I would be working with and felt very comfortable there. I couldn't wait to start. I believed my luck might be changing. The thought of a paycheck made me extremely happy.

· faux football ·

Tyler was playing football and summer practices had already begun. He loved football and had worked out for much of the past year to become stronger and quicker.

When double sessions started, Ty was home one day after the morning practice and had to skip the afternoon practice because of a dentist appointment. Once done, we headed over to my new office to bring up boxes of books and pictures. After a few minutes of helping, Ty asked me if I thought his right wrist looked swollen.

During morning football practice, his wrist had been caught between two players' helmets and he heard a snap. He hadn't said anything because he didn't want to hear that it was probably broken. An x-ray confirmed the break, and he was not able to play football for the entire season. He was crushed, but still made it to every single practice and game the whole season.

· scaring mice away ·

Some of the other patients in the radiation department were quiet people and kept to themselves. One woman in particular sat in a wheelchair every morning when I went in. Her very doting husband was always with her. Her head was down most of the time so the nurse in me tried to catch her eye. If I managed to, I would just smile at her. As time wore on, we eventually made small talk.

One day, I mentioned how her hair was coming back in nicely. She said she had emailed a picture of herself with no hair to her family. The picture also had a note on it that said she had used the same picture of herself on the fridge to scare mice away. She had a great sense of humor and smile, and I felt like I had accomplished something when we spoke. There is no reason to do this alone.

· off to see the wizard ·

*I*n a small room off the radiation room, the radiation technologists monitored their patients during treatment. It reminded me of the scene in the *Wizard of Oz* when the wizard was behind the curtain. The technician thought I was insane. Maybe I was.

· aloe ·

*J*ane told Brian that putting aloe gel on the radiated area immediately after treatment would improve the condition of my skin. I was prepared to have my skin burnt from the radiation. I hoped that I would not have to stop treatment for a few days if my skin burnt too much. My skin looked like it had a severe sunburn, but was okay otherwise.

I also learned to use deodorant "crystals" instead of regular deodorant, and use soap and lotions with no fragrance in them. Also, no underwire bras. I did every last thing that was recommended. There was an end in sight, and I was going to do everything that I could to get to the finish line.

· hitting the road ·

*B*ecause it was summer, when I came home from radiation treatments, the kids and I headed out to the lake or the beach. We also tried to go on a college tour every week for Travis. I had a new car and the miles added up pretty quickly.

When we toured one college, I wore my wig so I didn't draw attention to myself and the kids, but it was so windy on the campus that day that my wig blew all over the place!

· red sox ·

*M*y sister Karen and her husband had two extra tickets to a Red Sox game so they asked Brian and I to join them. They picked me up, we met Brian at work, and headed into Boston on a very humid night in July. I hadn't been to a game in a couple of years, even though I am an avid Red Sox fan.

Whenever I walk into Fenway Park, I remember the first time I went to a major league game. I was in the 2nd grade and my parents, Nana, and siblings had tickets to a game. We drove in to Boston and it was such an adventure for me.

I got choked up with emotion when I saw the lush green field and green monster. Nana was a *huge* Red Sox and Celtics fan, although she usually listened to the games on the radio.

Later that summer, Brian, the kids, and I were able to catch a Red Sox game. It was a great day in Boston together.

The day Jon Lester returned to the pitcher's mound for the Red Sox after a battle with lymphoma, was glorious for me. Here was a cancer survivor who had undergone months of chemo and had come back to pitch in the major leagues.

I was a bit choked up as he threw the first pitch. He made a statement that day by getting back out there that resonated around the world.

· fundraising ·

*F*rancie and I were invited to a benefit for the Pan Mass Challenge in honor of a friend's niece who had survived leukemia and was doing well. Francie was gracious enough to drive to Springfield and we called ourselves Pat and Chris from the old *Saturday Night Live* skits, because she wore her hair short and, for the moment, so did I.

We had a good night and chatted with quite a few people. I still felt like the elephant in the room, but, thankfully, I was slowly becoming a much smaller elephant.

· newport ·

My old neighbors were heading to Newport, Rhode Island, to spend the day at the beach. They invited us to join them and I looked forward to doing just that. After my radiation treatment that morning, I met them and we spent a great day at the beach. There were four adults and fourteen kids. The kids got along famously, and I was able to forget about treatment for a while.

· boob ·

_B_rian joked around about my poor breast. He originally dubbed it Franken Boob, then Fried Boob (during radiation), and finally Super Boob as the scar and burns faded quickly, and I looked very much like my old self. I was amazed at how my body healed.

· summer vacation ·

*E*very summer, our family spends a week at the beach with my in-laws. There are fifteen of us. That year, we decided that we were not going to go because we were unsure about when my treatment would end. My in-laws offered to take the kids so I could stay home and go to radiation and the kids wouldn't miss out on the annual trip with their cousins.

Brian and I went down a few days, and I drove down for the day when I really missed the kids. It worked out okay, but we never had a chance to relax as the summer sped by. Brian, the kids, and I did make it to the beach again for a day trip.

· the rest of the story ·

*W*hile the kids were at the beach, Brian and I headed out for dinner one evening. We stopped into a nearby Chinese restaurant and ran into Brian's childhood neighbors. They had to have noticed my extremely short hair, but they never said anything to me.

Later on, they stopped by my in-laws to make sure everything was okay with me. It was strange that so many people I knew had no idea about my diagnosis.

When I had my teeth cleaned, my hygienist asked if I had chosen to cut my hair like that. She has been my hygienist for over twenty years. When I told her the news, she answered that her mom had breast cancer and was doing well. I hadn't even thought there would be a second wave of people that I would have to tell. The difference this time, however, was that I was at the end of my treatment and it was easier to spread good news rather than uncertain news.

On my way home, I heard Barry Manilow's song, "I Made It Through the Rain" and I got choked up. It was a great tune to hear as I neared the finish line.

· what are words for? ·

*A*s a nurse, I never quite knew what to say to patients or family members who had been diagnosed with cancer. I thought having cancer myself would make me all-knowing, but I was wrong.

I was in the grocery store one day as my hair neared the pixie stage. A woman in the store was with her teenage son and wore a bandana to cover her bald head. I wanted to tell her that her hair would grow back and that she would soon feel more like herself. But I didn't. I didn't know if she would be okay, and I hated to interrupt her time with her son. It bothers me that I think I could be a positive role model and offer support to others living through this ordeal but I am not sure how to go about it.

· fresh start ·

I was scheduled to start my new job just two weeks after radiation treatment ended. I met with my boss and a colleague with whom I would be working very closely. Neither seemed fazed by my extreme hair makeover, even though I had worked with both of them in the past.

· biting my tongue ·

One of my meetings involved a prior classmate of mine with whom I had a class while undergoing chemotherapy. She only knew me with a wig and was never aware of my diagnosis.

As I arrived at the meeting, she said, "I thought Maryellen was coming."

I replied that it was me.

She then said, "Did you get a professional makeover? You got rid of that hair!" I chuckled to myself and later shared the story with my sisters and friends. They said I should have told her about my diagnosis just to see what her reaction would be. I preferred to stay under the radar on this one.

· returning to the human race ·

As the radiation ended, I walked out of the hospital with a feeling of relief that I had never known before. I had made it through and it was time to move on.

I shopped with the kids for their back-to-school clothes and supplies. I got back into the swing of work and can say that the ability to work a full day is truly a blessing. I had survived seventy-five trips to the doctor and hospital in eight months. I was elated to be back in the game of life!

· boat trip ·

$\mathcal{M}$y husband thought it would be a great idea to take his Dad's pontoon boat out on the lake for a day with my siblings and their spouses. There were eight of us embarking on the first annual boat trip. My brother and his wife were going to meet up with us when we docked the boat for dinner that evening. We looked like we were leaving on a year-long cruise! We had piles of snacks, coolers, and clothes. We had a blast.

We talked, laughed, drank, ate, and even managed to kneeboard on the lake. We had a lot of fun later, at the restaurant, even though the service was very slow. I can't wait for next year's trip.

· the five-year plan ·

*m*y follow-up appointment with the medical oncologist was scheduled for August 6th. It was the only August appointment that was available. August 6th was the day my father died twelve years before. I hoped it was a good omen. At that appointment, I was started on the medication Tamoxifen in pill form everyday for five years.

The side effects could include a stroke or blood clot, hot flashes, and a variety of other things. I was very hesitant to take this medication because of the side effects, but my oncologist said that the benefits of this thirty-year old medication outweighed the risks. I felt fine on this medication, and continued to take it without any problems.

· running ·

*M*y cousin Lynn decided to run the PF Chang Marathon in Arizona in January 2008. After consulting with my oncologist, I decided to train for it as well. I had begun to run again during radiation and was feeling pretty strong. After about three weeks into my training, I developed hip pain that I blamed on the chemotherapy. After undergoing tests, I found out that I had bursitis in my hip. My training stopped, and I decided to pace myself a bit more instead of barging into things head first. It was not going to be easy.

· first haircut ·

I didn't quite know what to do with my hair. It was growing in thick, soft, and wavy four months after the end of treatment. I have never appreciated anything quite as much as having my hair back. I needed a trim, and wasn't quite sure who to go to for my first haircut in over eight months. I called the local hair salon that cuts Brian and the kid's hair, because I had seen a plaque on their wall showing their participation in a local walk for breast cancer.

I told them about my chemo and hair, and they welcomed me and referred me to Barbara. Barbara was about my age and was amazingly compassionate. She had lost her mother to leukemia and was very empathetic to my experience. She trimmed the sides and back and was very supportive. I was grateful for the lack of fanfare. The fact that I needed a haircut was big enough news. Even though my hair resembled gosling down, I was so damn happy to have it back.

· returning to normal ·

One afternoon, I was talking to my sister Erin on my cell phone as I was approaching heavy traffic on my way to work. I told her how frustrated I was to be stuck in traffic and moving only a couple of yards every few minutes. We laughed because it was a beautiful thing to be upset about traffic. I had turned the corner and was finally starting to feel like myself. Boy, did it feel good.

· martin ·

Martin was christened on a beautiful Fall day. I was honored to be asked by Erin and Chris to be his godmother. I had come so far since the day he was born, and I had finished chemo. I thoroughly enjoyed little Martin's big day.

· new york, new york ·

I have wanted to go to New York City for as long as I can remember. When I was in high school, I even made a plan with some friends to run away to New York. Thankfully, the plan never got off the ground.

My NSBs and I decided to drive down and spend a weekend. I offered to drive because I had a new car and satellite radio. I had never driven into the city, but Moke and Francie had been there. The ride down was a breeze, and it seemed as if everything we touched turned to gold. We met amazing people, ate wonderful food, and scoured the city on foot and by cab. We took in all the sites and all the people. We walked, shopped, ate, laughed, talked, and then talked more. We felt as though we finally, although temporarily, had caught up with one another's lives. I hope to go back someday.

· people watching ·

I have always been drawn to watching people and trying to figure out what they may be thinking. When I was a kid, I watched people in their cars on the highway. I tried to gauge whether they were happy with their passengers or not. I created stories about where they might be going or from where they came.

I realized at a young age that there were a lot of sad people out there. People were not always coming from exciting places. People were on their way to and from doctor's offices after hearing bad news, rushing to hospitals after learning that their loved one was in an accident, had a difficult day at work, or had a fight with a family member or friend.

One day when I was only about five or six years old, I saw a very elderly woman with an eye patch and cataract glasses on in a car that we passed, and it made me realize that we all have to cut people some slack. I also realized that a smile was like magic. If we happened to pass a car and the driver smiled at me, I suddenly felt better. Then I would smile back.

· the office ·

My new office on campus was a bright corner office with cell phone reception. It was the same office I had borrowed six months prior on the day that I was evaluating students and running around for my MRI report before I was officially diagnosed. This time, the office had a more positive vibe.

· coming out of the closet ·

I loved my new job and was about six weeks into it when I decided to let my co-workers know about my diagnosis and let them know how I spent the first eight months of 2007. I wasn't quite sure who knew and who didn't, so I figured I'd clear the air. The email I sent was as follows:

Because it is October, I have decided, after much deliberation, to share my story with you. Please keep in mind that I prefer to live my life "under the radar" and with as little attention as possible (must be because I'm a middle child!)

Last December I was diagnosed with breast cancer. After spending the first 8 months of 2007 receiving treatment for my diagnosis (no, this is *not* my hairdo of choice!), I am healthy and am told that I will live a long life. Lucky you!

I am hoping that by sharing my story with you—that you and everyone that you know will be sure to receive screening (since I think we're all over 40!) and be aware of any changes in ourselves.

I had <u>ABSOLUTELY NO</u> risk factors for this disease—no family history—I have always exercised as I have been a runner for 28 years—don't drink often (unless it's a really bad week!), and eat well. My point is that we are quick to postpone or delay our doctor appointments because we are so busy, but it is important that we take care of ourselves. It is the most important thing we can do.

October is Breast Cancer Awareness month (I'm so tired of the pink ribbons already!) but if it allows us to have an awareness of the disease and spread the word to the women AND men in our lives, it is worth being inundated with pink for a while.

I am honored to be part of such a great group of colleagues!

Back to business as usual,

—MARYELLEN

· feedback ·

I received positive responses from everyone I worked with. The department chair said I did a great job. I told her that I felt like I was coming
out of the closet, and that I couldn't move forward until I told my story. I
was pleasantly surprised at their reaction and I felt a weight lifted from
my shoulders.

· guest lecture ·

I was invited by a colleague to be a guest lecturer in her Chronic Illness class. She thought that it would be helpful for seasoned nurses to hear about the affects of this disease on every level of a person's life. I was happy to speak of my experience, and have oftentimes thought that I would like to volunteer as a spokesperson for an organization or run a support group.

I wrote out key points that I wished to discuss and found the experience exhilarating and extremely exhausting.

· is that really you? ·

I saw people during treatment that either didn't recognize me, or chose to ignore me. I didn't care either way, but I thought that I might not look the same as I did before. My eyes were not as bright and, well, there was the thing about my hair. After my hair grew back and my eyes regained their twinkle, however, people did recognize me again. The whole thing was very strange.

I no longer have a second wind. At the end of a long day, I can't rally like I used to, and the great thing is that I don't care. If I put in a full day, when it is time to crash, I crash.

· ph.d or rv ? ·

*D*uring the spring, I applied to a Nursing Ph.D program. I was torn about whether I wanted to go back to school and get back on the academic treadmill, trying to balance work, family, and classes. Even after I was accepted into a program, I thought long and hard about returning. Should I go for my Ph.D or rent an RV and go cross-country and have some fun?

I accepted the spot in the Ph.D program. I had lived my life with a "full steam ahead" approach and wasn't going to change. I loved the fact that I was back and fully engaged in life again. I would always love spending time with my husband and kids as they grew into adulthood, laugh with my friends and family, and be a lifelong teacher and student.

I did a small project in one of my Ph.D classes about women's experiences with the side effects from breast cancer treatment. I hope I can do further research in this area.

· one year later ·

*A*s I approached my forty-second birthday and the anniversary of my diagnosis, I had learned a great deal about myself and others. I am a good person, and my strengths as well as my weaknesses are blessings. I am still overwhelmed by the support that I have received and am very aware of how many people love me. I now know that if I ever need anything, there are bands of people who would help me anywhere and at any time.

I am also grateful to those who care for cancer patients every day. I am amazed by all they do to alleviate fear, encourage laughter, and make a difficult time bearable with their expertise and compassion.

I also realize that my children are kind and compassionate, as well as resilient. They also have fantastic senses of humor. For these characteristics and all of their other incredible attributes, I am proud.

I have also been fortunate to have been given the opportunity to teach a new generation of nurses. I am aware that I have a lot to learn about teaching, but I can honestly say that I have found my calling in life. I hope the students agree. The next forty-two years of my life will be lived much like my first forty-two. Well, almost. I will smile more, love more deeply, and ride around in my car with the windows down and my hair flying in the breeze.

· follow-up ·

*I*continue to experience follow up appointments and testing as very
stressful. I am aware that if a result comes back as less than perfect,
my life can change on a dime. I am not worried everyday, but feel anxious
when appointments near.

Two years after I was first diagnosed, the nurse practitioner found a
lump in the opposite breast. My life stopped. I was cruising along with my
life when I realized again how much it could change within a few short
weeks. I had a mammogram, ultrasound, MRI, and fine needle aspiration
of the new lump over the course of several weeks.

The holiday season was coming, and I wondered whether the worry of
a recurrence would be with me for a lifetime. Everything turned out fine,
but I was stopped short for several weeks by fear.

· in defense of the color pink ·

I am beginning to think that I was a little hard on the color pink. I have nothing against pink anymore. After a short hiatus, I have begun to see pink as my favorite color again.

Pink equals strength. Pink reminds me of how far I have come since that day when the phone rang with the news. Pink grounds me and allows me to realize all that I have to be grateful for.

To be inundated with *pink reminders* when facing this diagnosis was overwhelming to me at first. October can be especially difficult because there are pink ribbons *everywhere*. It is hard to forget about having had breast cancer during the month of October.

But I see pink a little differently now. It raises awareness, and that is exactly what is needed to prevent and beat this disease. If one woman or man decides to have a mammogram or do a self-breast exam because of advertisements, then pink is doing its job.

I still think that I will be hard pressed to wear anything with a pink ribbon on it that brings attention to me, but I will continue to contribute to the effort for awareness by telling my story and supporting those causes that are close to my heart.

· the future ·

*T*o me, the future looks bright. I am healthy, productive, and happy. I will probably have sleepless nights as follow up appointments near. But I continue to live my life after treatment the same way that I did during treatment. If I do the best I can everyday, there is nothing else I can ask of myself.